AGED TO PERFECTION

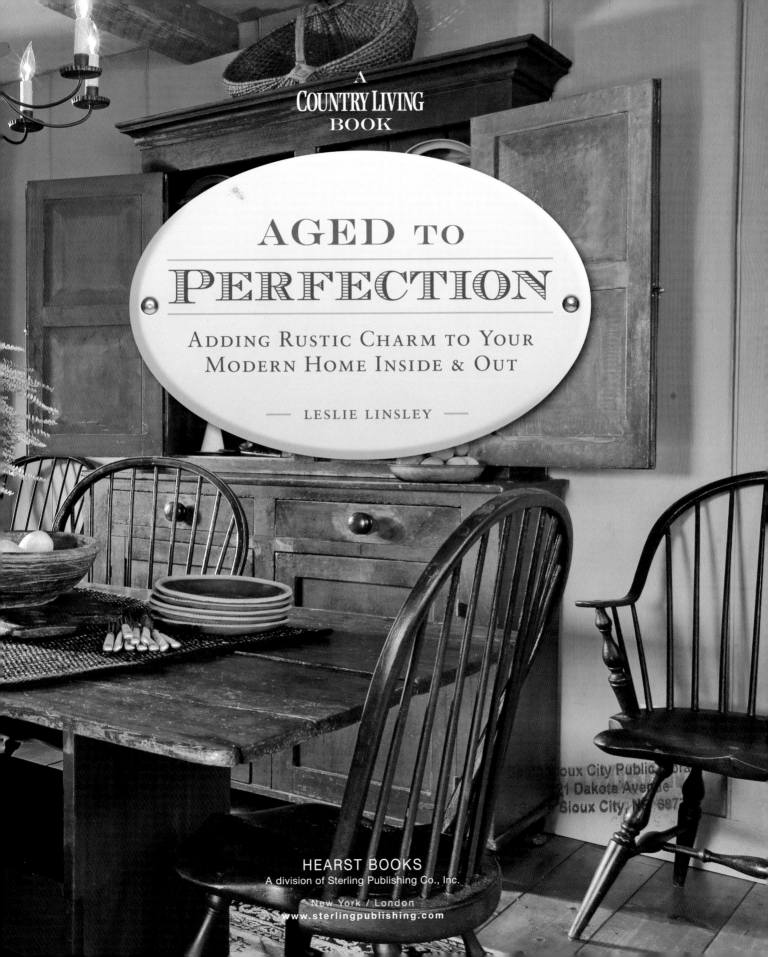

A
COUNTRY LIVING
BOOK

AGED TO PERFECTION

ADDING RUSTIC CHARM TO YOUR MODERN HOME INSIDE & OUT

— LESLIE LINSLEY —

HEARST BOOKS
A division of Sterling Publishing Co., Inc.

New York / London
www.sterlingpublishing.com

C O N T

3

4

INTRODUCTION

There is something wonderful and romantic about an older home, one with timeless character that exudes the feeling of being lived in for generations. The gracious houses constructed in Colonial times, for example, were classic in style and often built with techniques and materials that are no longer employed. We love visiting someone who lives in an older home built in the 1800s; living in one is, however, quite another matter.

People often romanticize an old home, but buying one may require renovations—like putting in new kitchen and bathrooms and upgrading plumbing and heating systems—that can be costly. Similarly, the rooms in older homes were often built small to conserve heat, so interior walls must often be removed to make the house more livable by modern standards. Fortunately, it is easy to bring the charming characteristics of an old house to our new homes: architectural details such as chair rails, exposed beams, floor and ceiling moldings, window and door trims, window panes of leaded glass, and worn, wooden floorboards can all give a new home the character of an older house.

I live on Nantucket Island off the coast of Cape Cod in Massachusetts, where there are more historic homes built in the 1700s and 1800s than in any other town in the United States. (There are even some houses built in the 1600s!) For the most part, these homes have been restored and are maintained as they might have been centuries ago.

The window and mantle trim are all painted a Colonial shade of green.

Having written many books documenting how these homeowners have renovated and redesigned these houses for today's lifestyles, I'm acutely aware of their wonderful characteristics—as well as their inefficiencies.

While we may want the character of an old home, we also want the contemporary feeling that attracted us to buy or build a new one. New houses usually offer more space and features than older homes. They are built with modern conveniences and more efficient infrastructures. However, they often lack the architectural details that make older homes so appealing.

Think of your new home as a blank canvas just waiting for a patina of "older home appeal." All across America, homeowners have turned new houses into charming studies of earlier nineteenth century homes reflective of their area. Furniture, paint, fabric, window treatments, accessories, and architectural details are the basic ingredients that go into making a new house ooze charm and creating a lived-in feeling—one that is surprisingly easy to achieve. In the end, you'll have the best of both worlds: a new old house.

This combination of the old and the new is what gives our rooms personality. Decorators know that an eclectic mix of furnishings yields the most beautiful results, and there are many advantages to furnishing a new home with antiques, collectibles, and accessories from the past, such as quilts. Comfort comes from using old pieces, and there is much value in giving old things new life. An older chair, table, sideboard, armoire, or sofa can be integrated with modern pieces to give a room character: a modern home decorated with older pieces of furniture is far more interesting than one that sports a matching set of anything.

Almost everyone has something they've inherited from relatives. Some of this furniture might have been accepted because it helped to save money. Some of it might be cherished. Either way, old furniture will keep a new house from seeming, well, new. (If the furniture you inherited isn't in good shape, it can be restored, as long as its structure is basically sound: where there's a good design, there's a way to make it work.) And if you haven't been the lucky recipient of heirloom furniture, you should try antique shops, flea markets, and yard sales for great places to locate what you need. Reproductions of Early American furniture are easily found and quite affordable. The trick is to give traditional pieces of furniture a youthful energy so the house doesn't look as though it was decorated by accident, with odds and ends. To make old pieces seem fresh, mix in new accessories, like modern lamps and art. You might use an old four-poster bed but cover it with linens as fresh as tomorrow, with colors that reflect contemporary tastes.

Aside from architectural details, recycled furniture, collections, and salvaged materials, you can use paint, stains, wallpaper, fabrics, and window treatments to make a new house look old. Sometimes the right choice of colors is all that is needed to make rooms exciting or elegant. This applies to the walls and trim around windows and doors, but furniture, too, can be reclaimed with a coat of paint in a color most often found in old homes.

Historic paint colors reflect not only the natural pigments colonists worked with but also how colors were perceived in earlier times: by candlelight, through small or heavily draped windows, and browned by smoke and age. In the Colonial era, paint was scarce, so walls were often whitewashed, with color reserved for the trim. Colonial green was popular for wainscoting, or the bottom half of a wall. Barn red was a shade associated with wealth and typically found in public rooms; it shows up on cupboards and other pieces of furniture as well. Earthy pigments of gold were more common and, in the eighteenth century, used mostly in private quarters. Federal blue was an important interior color in the eighteenth century as well, used in living or dining rooms. Today it is often a favorite for the bedroom.

The houses in this book represent a diverse mix chosen from various parts of the country. They demonstrate a creative approach to the reinterpretation of architectural details and interior furnishings in the best new homes today. Let them inspire you to make your new home look aged to perfection.

The inside of this cupboard is a typical milk paint shade of blue.

{ 1 }

BUILDING OLD

Older homes in the United States are often distinguishable by their architectural style—details such as shutters, windows, and doors, as well as the materials used in their construction. When planning the building of your house, there are many easy ways to give it characteristics associated with older homes.

Before beginning construction on a new house, seek out older homes in your area. Look through magazines and books to get ideas for building old. Check out the Web sites of architects and builders in your area. In other words, do your research before you start. Consider incorporating period details into the design and employing materials that were used long ago to make your new house look old. For example, you might look in salvage shops for an old front door, use reproduction square nails on wide pine floorboards, and choose divided-light, double-hung windows.

What one person dismisses as junk another might see as the beginning of something beautiful. Many homeowners thrive on discovering new ways to use abandoned objects. It can be a challenge to build with repurposed materials. For example, you can often find old windows and doors at garage sales and use them strategically in a new room. One homeowner lined her ceiling with old wooden doors to add geometry and the warmth of painted wood. Salvaged chestnut or pine flooring, large ceiling beams, stone for entryway flooring or surrounding a fireplace, and antique

Shades of gold and yellow reflect an earlier time as do elaborate mirror and picture frames, silk lamp shades, old photos and memorabilia.

A mix of fabric on sumptuous pillow creates a cozy, comfortable look on the sofa.

materials that have stood the test of time will surely add more character to your home than something brand new. If you mix repurposed materials (such as worn floorboards and perhaps barn board) for building an addition to your existing home, it will be hard to tell that your house was newly built.

Older homes were built with plaster, not drywall. When planning the construction of your house, consider skim coating the walls in plaster (rather than using bland sheetrock—a dead giveaway that a house is new) to give the rooms solidity. Historically, there was a great deal of color on painted wood. The walls, floors, and cabinets of older houses were often painted in shades of blues and greens, with a patina and depth that can be achieved through layering, rubbing, and glazing.

There are many things you can do to create the feeling of elegance associated with gracious older homes: a second-floor balcony, a wraparound porch, a large front door flanked by sidelights with transom windows above, or French doors across an entire wall in a living room. Copies of early twelve-over-twelve paned windows are produced to look like the originals but function better, with double panes for insulation and double-hung screens. Recessed ceiling lights are often used in modern home construction but are never found in older homes. While lamplight is much warmer and creates coziness, for practicality, you might consider recessed ceiling lights in the kitchen and use table

hardware are just some examples of reclaimed and recycled materials; previously used for other purposes, they can be part of a most effective approach to building today.

After you've done your research you can plan every detail, right down to a deliberately crooked or slanted floor, so that your newly built and furnished home resembles a house that has been in the family for generations. Once you have the blueprints for your house, take them with you wherever you go. Scour antique shops, salvage outlets, and online sources and look at historic homes in your area or wherever you travel. Search for weathered beams, brass doorknobs—even old nails and hinges with a handcrafted pedigree. Beyond their intrinsic beauty, lamps as auxiliary lighting on counters when task light isn't necessary.

While there is definite charm and character in an old house, there are advantages to building new; modern appliances and plumbing and windows that work properly are among them. Many manufacturers of bathroom accessories offer reproductions of early styles, and while they aren't antiques, they look like (and usually function much better than) the originals. The Kohler Company, for example, makes a steeping tub that has the look of an early claw-foot tub. Using a light, whitewashed cupboard to replace a medicine cabinet on bead board walls will result in a charming bathroom with a nod to the nineteenth century.

While the interior of your rooms might look rustic, you want everything to function perfectly, using the latest and best technology, so consider planning ways to hide appliances by covering them with reclaimed material or housing them in cabinets that look old. For example, a dishwasher and trash compacter might fit nicely inside a cabinet fitted with bin pulls from an old apothecary.

Colonial blue was a favorite paint color in early dining rooms.

DECORATING STYLES

Some homeowners are devoted to a certain period of furnishings and are sticklers for authenticity. They prefer Early American or European influences and enjoy looking for pieces that fulfill a desire to express these styles in all the rooms of their home. Still others like the mix-and-match approach, and their homes reflect a more eclectic aesthetic. When deciding how to furnish your home, consider your lifestyle. Do you want your home to be relaxed and casual or formal? Do you favor a country farmhouse feeling or something more elegant? Do you want to mix furniture that is old and new, or do you want everything authentic and from a specific period?

Aqua green paint suggests a vintage kitchen in a modern home.

Period Style

Many homeowners are fascinated with history and enjoy decorating their homes with furniture that expresses a specific historical period. While Early American is most popular for decorating with a country feeling, furniture from other historical periods can create a more formal look that gives a new house old-world character. These rooms often combine a rich color palette with antiques and collections about which the homeowner is passionate. Pieces in the Louis XV and XVI styles, particularly painted items, infuse a home with a certain romantic spirit.

The art of collecting antique furniture enhances one's knowledge of history. If this is your passion, consider imbuing antique furnishings with a fresh look by incorporating traditional but newly manufactured fabrics like ticking, toile, and classic floral prints that might have graced the furniture originally. The accessories and collectibles you use to personalize your rooms might be an assortment of ironstone, candlesticks, portraits, mirrors, and paintings that pull your house back in time and make it feel both perfect for today and respectful of the past.

When it comes to color, blue and yellow is the classic palette for a period style, but you can introduce brighter hues as well. For example, you might be inspired to use lush fabrics, mixing them the way it was done in the seventeenth and eighteenth centuries. During that period, expensive yardage was used to cover the interior of a chair, while less expensive fabric was used to cover the outside. Chairs can make a simple room interesting, and this is a wonderful way to make over a chair with good lines but of no particular lineage—and you'll get a luxurious look with just a small amount of fabric.

A Fortuny fabric panel, a 1901 sink with a fluted column base, and an assortment of antique frames and architectural elements give the bathroom old-world elegance.

Have the confidence to marry different styles and periods with contemporary reproductions. Hang portraits from the 1800s and 1900s to add romance and a bit of mystery to your rooms. (An unsuspecting visitor might even wonder if the paintings' subjects once inhabited your house!) Finishing touches such as this make it easy to forget that your home was newly built.

The rich combination of citrus colors in the guest bedroom is reminiscent of Tuscany.

Every detail of the furnishings is carefully chosen and given plenty of breathing room. The light colors enhance the openness of the floor plan. A black mannequin's shape, size, and color make it an interesting accessory for the corner of the room.

Cream-colored homespun fabrics are used on upholstered furniture and create a soft contrast with the occasional primitive pieces.

Vintage Revival

Vintage style—commonly called shabby chic—originated in Great Britain during the Victorian era, between 1830 and 1901. As a popular decorative style today, it evokes the type of decoration found in large country houses, with their worn and faded old chintz sofas and curtains, old paintwork, and unassuming good taste. Recycling old furniture and fabrics is an important aspect of the look. The early forms of shabby chic were rather grand, but the style has evolved, taking inspiration from eighteenth-century Swedish painted furnishings, the French château, and even the American Shakers, for whom simplicity and plainness were essential. Popular décor items are pillows made of vintage bark cloth, old linens, chenille bedspreads, vintage chandeliers, and anything with roses on it. It is a soft, relaxed, feminine, romantic way of decorating that looks comfortable and inviting.

The essence of vintage style is antique furniture heavily painted white (or a soft pastel color), with many layers showing through obviously worn areas or distressed at the corners by sanding. The style can easily be imitated in faux painting by using glaze or by painting and then rubbing and sanding away the top coat to show the wood or base coats.

Layers of texture also define this style, especially when creating a romantic bedroom: fabrics establish a sense of cozy comfort layer by layer. Consider a flouncy bed skirt, pillows covered with old tapestry and antique lace, and draperies made from linen tablecloths. *Bleached* and *faded* are words often applied to vintage style fabrics, which tend toward cotton and linen, with linen (inspired by old French linens) being particularly popular. Whites and worn or bleached out pastels (like pink, mint green, and pale aqua) are favorite colors. New fabric is often stained with tea to give it the look of old fabric.

Accessories used in vintage-style decorating come from Early American

Painted furnishings in grayed blues and red, such as a William and Mary chest and small apothecary, add color with an appealing patina. As a rule, a reproduction chest of drawers functions better than an original, but mixing in some genuine antiques, such as a blanket chest or night table, helps root the reproductions in authenticity.

Red walls in a study are the one exception to an all-white home. Metal security gates are now bulletin boards, and an old restaurant prep table serves as a desk.

A bedroom sanctuary is appointed with antique pine, sturdy enamelware, wind-up clocks, a *matelassé* coverlet, and faded rose-printed pillow cases that have a European flair. Each landscape features an idyllic cottage. A painted shutter creates an interesting headboard for the bed.

ephemera, a word that derives from the Greek, literally meaning something that isn't meant to last—something designed to be short-lived—it is also a general term used to describe collections of minor documents of everyday life. Ephemera were usually created for a specific, limited purpose and generally intended for discard after use. But such transient, workaday items from the past have become keepsakes and are used as an unpretentious, stylish way to decorate. Often they include printed material that conveys content of some topical importance, such as advertisements, tickets, menus, forms, invitations, bookmarks, ballots, greeting cards, postcards, and the like—materials that were created for a single practical purpose, with no thought that they would be saved or preserved. Ephemera define vintage style perfectly. Flea markets, secondhand shops, and antique stores across America overflow with ephemera,

as there is no limit to the appeal of vintage revival as a charming way to add a bit of history and character to any home.

Vintage style is defined by an aesthetic that combines worldly glamour with a wistful nostalgia. It's a less-than-serious look often created with surroundings that can be enjoyed for the moment and then changed on a whim. The best results come from combining the old and the new, curious and surprising treasures, casual furnishings and unexpectedly beautiful oddities. It takes experience to learn how to mix old and new pieces to create interesting rooms, but it's a knack that can be developed through trial and error. As you acquire vintage things you will find yourself putting them together in different ways until you come upon an arrangement that pleases you. The thing to remember is that there are no rules: the fun is in the discovery of what goes together to create a casual environment that doesn't look haphazard.

It might start with a painting or an old mirror to place on the wall; all sorts of interesting objects to hold dressing table items might follow. These containers may have had other uses and come from different periods. Before you know it your first pieces are dictating others. The more vintage items you arrange together, the better the whole vignette becomes. Remember to put favorite objects where you spend the most time. In this way, being at home will always be a pleasure because you will be surrounded by the things you love most.

Mismatched chairs and pieces of architectural details are chosen over matching sets of furniture and paintings purchased to match the sofa. Curtains might be handmade from vintage dishtowels or embroidery-edged pillowcases. Collections are varied and play a big

part in the overall scheme of the design. More often proves to be better than less, as vintage decorating tends to eschew editing. There always seems to be room for one more lace-edged pillow or a lovely pitcher of fresh flowers on a dresser already filled with rosebud vases of varying sizes. When it comes to personal style, everything goes, with few restrictions. If it's worn and white, soft green, faded pink, or has delicate flowers on it, the rule of mix and match is embraced with abandon.

Floors tend to be mostly bare with a few hooked, braided, or needlepoint rugs. (No wall-to-wall carpeting, ever!) Old plates, frames, and mirrors are favorite accessories to hang on walls. But not everything has to be old. It's good to be able to spot a great new-but-old-looking item at discount stores. Remember, anything that is inherently well designed can be elevated to the status of your other furnishings once it has been removed from the discount-store environment. Restaurant supply shops also provide good "pickin's" for decorators: using industrial materials alongside soft furnishings and paint-worn, wooden items can also be quite interesting.

Where does one find vintage furnishings that can fulfill a vision so perfectly and make one's home into a personal statement? Many devoted homeowners spend a lot of time on eBay to find the collections and furnishings from a certain period or style. Others mix newly purchased items with treasures

Apples look especially inviting in a rustic, paint-worn box.

Matelassé coverlets and pillow shams are often used to create a vintage-style bedroom that has a romantic, old-world feeling. The word *matelassé* means "quilted" or "padded" fabric in French. It is often a hand-stitched textile, similar to a type of quilt made in Provence. *Matelassé* fabric is commonly made of cotton and appears quite elegant. It is favored for its comfortable, casual design and improves with each washing. The textile is a favorite for shabby-chic and French provincial décor. Antique and heirloom *matelassé* can be found in antique stores and online through individual collectors. New *matelassé* coverlets are readily available through catalogs and home furnishings stores. After a few washings they become as soft as antique quilts and look every bit as good.

from their family, and still others haunt antique shops and secondhand stores, wouldn't consider missing a yard sale, and travel far and wide to swap meets and flea markets to find what they covet. For them, bargain hunting becomes a favorite activity, and beloved haunts are visited on a regular basis. Many homeowners who have taken the time to furnish their homes in this way say that when every piece you own tells a story, it has special meaning and will provide you with a sense of place so you will never tire of being at home.

TIPS FOR BARGAIN HUNTING

1. Visit favorite destinations frequently. New items often arrive on a daily basis.
2. Build relationships with stores and dealers you like so they will call when something that might interest you comes in.
3. Travel farther afield. Make periodic buying trips to favorite places.
4. Not everything has to be old. With practice, you can search places like Ikea, Marshalls, and T.J. Maxx for potentially old-looking items that have a vintage look.
5. Don't forgo something just because it no longer works as intended due to its fragility; simply find a gentler use for it. For example, a rickety bench might be used to hold blankets, a quilt, or linens at the end of a bed, or be piled with books.
6. Old plates may be chipped or faded, but they make terrific wall art. Look for colors and patterns that go together. Mismatched plates are easy to find for very little money in thrift shops and at yard sales. Mix old and new, or group together different styles in one color for an interesting look.

HOW TO CREATE VINTAGE ACCESSORIES

Vintage Wall Clock: To make a cherry print wall clock: 1. Remove the paper face from a cheap plastic wall clock. 2. Use this to cut a piece of cherry print of the same size from fabric or scrapbook paper and insert it into the same position in the clock. 3. Paint the outside bright red with acrylic paint.

Retro Seat Cushions: Another way to decorate your kitchen with a retro cherry print design is to re-cover kitchen chairs with the fabric. You will need a staple gun and fabric slightly larger than the seat. Paint the chairs mint green before re-covering the seats.

Café Curtains: Make café curtains from tea towels. No sewing is required. Simply attach clip-on curtain rings evenly spaced across one short end.

To age fabric, such as a slipcover for an upholstered chair, use RIT dye in Tan. Set the washing machine on the hottest setting, add the dye and salt, and allow it to agitate until the dye dissolves. Turn off the machine and soak the fabric, making sure it is completely submerged.

Classic Country

Classic country style, both an attitude and a lifestyle, represents our roots. It is a way of life from the past, perhaps the way our grandparents or great-grandparents lived in America. The word *country* might conjure up a little Cape Cod with a central chimney, steeply pitched roof, and two pairs of windows on either side of a front door—like a child's first drawing of a house. Another classic American country house is the saltbox, a lean-to structure that sprouted what in Nantucket are called "warts," or additions to

A two-hundred-year-old iron handle from an antique store opens the door of a Sub-Zero fridge clad in reclaimed wood—the perfect marriage of old and new.

Above: Cheery quilts are displayed on both the bed and a traditional quilt rack in the room's far corner.

Below: The shingle and Missouri limestone exterior includes such elegant details as a second-floor balcony and a large front door flanked by sidelights and a transom.

Missouri limestone was used on the floor of the entryway for practicality and its good looks. The walls are painted sunny ochre, which is also found on the wonderful old pine table. An antique hooked rug is hung as art on the wall.

accommodate growing families. Other classic country-style homes were the New England farmhouses and stone farmhouses built by Dutch settlers in New York and New Jersey, and the log cabin construction in the Midwest.

Some details to consider using are weathered outdoor bricks in front of a hearth, vintage doors, wide-plank wood flooring, and kitchen countertops crafted from salvaged wood floors.

Twelve-over-twelve window panes and transom windows over the doorway are typical of early homes in this country and are reminiscent of Federal-style architecture.

This grandly proportioned living room is bathed in sunlight from the nearly floor-to-ceiling windows and French doors on three sides. Salvaged chestnut floorboards and beams add warmth to the room.

Cabin Style

When one thinks of early homes in this country, Aspen, Colorado, isn't the first place that comes to mind. However, reclaimed lumber, salvaged stone, and antique hardware, along with carefully chosen furnishings and paint colors make this new house in the Rocky Mountains look and feel like one of the original homesteads built in this area around 1897. The cabin-style house is made almost entirely of materials once used for other purposes that have been reclaimed and recycled and demonstrates how effective this approach to building can be.

By mixing repurposed materials such as rough-hewn beams and worn floorboards from a house in Maine, and reconstructing a 150-year-old oak cabin as a bedroom, it's hard to tell that the house was built just one year ago. The furnishings also speak of an earlier age that symbolizes comfort and an informal lifestyle. Every detail is personal and steeped in history so that when you cross the threshold of this new-old house, you get an instant feeling of home.

Reclaimed lumber, salvaged stone, and a corrugated tin roof make a new house feel like an 1890s homestead.

One of the clever details in the kitchen is a vegetable sink made from an old brass bucket set into a granite-topped island.

The hallway leading to the breezeway and master bedroom is deliberately crooked, just as it might be in an early home. The blue shutters slide across the window of a family office.

Massive beams came from an old factory in Oregon and hold aloft the pitched ceiling in the living room. The ceiling color was achieved by layering the red paint for depth.

Modern Country

What is modern country style? It can best be described as a house with all the charm of a nineteenth century country home and a fresh exuberance that comes from an open floor plan, high ceilings, top-of-the-line fixtures, and appliances that are well designed. It might even have a bit of sophistication owing to oversize doors and windows that let lots of light into the rooms. While the rooms in a typical country house might be small and traditionally laid out, the modern country home incorporates bathrooms and kitchens that are designed a bit more spaciously but use materials such as bead board on the walls, wainscoting around a dining room wall, and even exposed rafters with the insulation on the outside. A new house can be given country charm with plenty of unexpected old-house details such as weathered outdoor bricks in front of a fireplace hearth, vintage doors, wide-plank wood flooring, and kitchen countertops crafted from salvaged wood floors or soapstone (a material used at the turn of the eighteenth century paired with oversized porcelain sinks instead of the more modern granite and stainless steel combo.)

A 1940s house in California is injected with old-house character by using subtle but significant details. The vintage fireplace mantel, for example, retains its original paint; outdoor brick was used for the hearth.

Small, dark rooms were replaced with an open airy floor plan. A white flower garden provides freshen cut flowers that are perfectly suited to every room.

Bead board and antique brackets add country details in the kitchen. A collection of white chinaware provides a refreshingly crisp country feeling.

Glass kitchen cabinets reveal a collection of white pottery and clear glasses that faithfully adhere to the neutral color scheme. Kitchen countertops are crafted from salvaged wood floors. You would never know that the pulley lights are reproductions—and therefore function better than the originals.

New England Saltbox

At the turn of the eighteenth century, the saltbox house was a familiar sight dotting the New England landscape. Traditionally, the saltbox has two stories in the front but just one in the back, giving it the long, pitched roof sloping down to the back that distinguishes this simple, wood-frame house. (A central chimney is another recognizable feature.) Its name comes from its shape, which resembles a wooden, lidded box in which salt was once kept. The style was popular for structures throughout the Colonial period because of the simplicity of its design.

Saltboxes, along with many other types of Colonial houses, are considered timber-frame houses. Timber-frame construction was, in fact, the method of building all frame houses in the seventeenth and eighteenth centuries in America, when the abundance of wood made the timber frame popular. The exterior of a saltbox was often finished with clapboard or other wooden siding.

This tidy red saltbox standing on a wooded lot in Massachusetts was built just eleven years ago but appears to have been here for centuries. The color of the house paint is a custom-mixed blend and is reminiscent of the color of original saltbox houses built in the seventeenth and eighteenth centuries.

This classic East Coast–style saltbox was actually built in the state of Washington in 1997. The house reflects the definitive saltbox profile: a two-story rectangular dwelling of unembellished clapboard with a steeply pitched roof angling to a single story at the rear. The stripped wooden door is flanked on each side by an onion lamp, a staple on Early American homes. Two-over-two transom windows top the doorway.

Reclaimed bricks from an old factory were used to create the living room floor, and hand-hewn beams and barn boards were used on the ceiling—two outstanding features that give the living room character. The furnishings bring a sense of Massachusetts's history to this new home.

A keeping room is an area just off the kitchen of a home and dates back to Colonial times, when families would sleep in that area when the rest of the house was cold. Wide plank pine floors, installed by the owners, have mellowed over time to a rich pumpkin shade.

The Sunday House

Sprinkled throughout the Texas Hill Country are charming one-hundred-year-old homes called Sunday houses. Built by German-American farmers and ranchers who came to town on Saturday for supplies and spent the night in order to go to church the next day, Sunday houses were small second homes with outside staircases that helped conserve space. Many of these early houses can be found in Fredericksburg, Texas. Their wonderful features can be adapted to make a new home just as charming. Among these characteristics are a wraparound porch and rooms opening to the outdoors, which add to the feeling of space.

Fashioned after the one-hundred-year-old Sunday houses sprinkled throughout the Texas Hill Country, this house is just ten years old. The front porch, with its supporting posts topped with Texas star carved ornamentation, is one of the features that attracted its new owner.

The master bedroom was a 150-year-old cabin in Missouri in another life. It was deconstructed and then reconstructed and is authentic down to its wide, painted floorboards.

A New Addition to Look Old

Sometimes it's easier to build from scratch than to add onto an old house and then try to give the addition the same aged feeling of the original part. But many people have done this quite successfully, doubling their square footage and at the same time being faithful to the original house.

A peaked ceiling framed in antique beams, unadorned symmetrically placed windows, painted wide pine floorboards, and bead board interior walls are some of the features you might consider to infuse a new addition with an old soul. When adding onto an old home, the new part should be in proportion to the old part of the house—the two should meld seamlessly. You should not be able to tell where the old ends and the new begins.

Farmhouse Style

Farmhouse architecture is most recognizable by its basic design elements, including covered porches, dormer windows, and white paint. Heavy stone and timber were predominant in regions where these natural materials were readily available. Classic forms and details from the Greek Revival, Georgian, and Victorian architectural eras were all incorporated into farmhouse architecture. These design elements were, however, simplified to accommodate more modest means.

Farmhouse style is similar to a country house; the main difference is that a farmhouse usually has a porch that wraps around the home. The roof ridge runs parallel to the street, with or without dormers. The roof slopes to a shallow pitch at the porch. One main roof covers the main body of the home. The exterior material is clapboard siding.

American farmhouse architecture embodied the need for basic comfort and was both practical and pleasant in its design. These sturdy and well-crafted

Salvaged materials, like green nineteenth-century raised-panel shutters, help create the illusion of a New England farmhouse in another time and place. The raised-seam metal roof has its color "baked in, adobe-like look," and thus requires no maintenance.

homes were built to last. Formal spaces were generally positioned at the front of the house, while spaces for daily chores were placed at the back. These family homesteads often began very modest in size and scale, evolving to have larger, more sprawling footprints as families grew and wealth increased. Random outcroppings and winglike additions are indicative of the historic transformations these homesteads experienced over time.

The objects you use to accessorize should function rather than simply be ar-ranged for looks. Clothes might hang from wall pegs, because these houses rarely had an abundance of closets. Practicality best describes farmhouse style: worn painted furniture, claw-foot tubs, deep porcelain kitchen sinks, bead board-covered walls, wide pine board floors, a butcher-block table in the kitchen, plate racks holding earthenware, a cupboard filled with pew-ter dishes and banded bowls, and perhaps bunches of dried lavender hanging from a rafter or beam. Never ornate, farmhouse style is a plain and straightforward design.

The interior walls of this house were once the exterior siding on both a barn and a chicken coop. The wood siding was sim-ply cleaned off by power washing and nailed to the walls for a beautifully aged texture.

Beginning with the floors, the owners were able to find enough salvaged heart pine to cover the entire first floor, which is left bare except for the living room area carpet. The interior walls are painted white to create a feeling of space and provide a backdrop for the individual furniture pieces and creative salvaged "art."

GETTING THE COUNTRY FARMHOUSE LOOK

One of the best things about the country farmhouse look is that it is relatively inexpensive to create. It's all about maximizing the potential of the things you already have. There are also many opportunities for purchasing low-cost pieces in this style at flea markets and local arts-and-crafts fairs. Before you start buying, though, be sure to check out your own belongings first. You may find you have been hiding away a whole new look for your home in all of those old family hand-me-downs.

New homebuilders and home renovators are experiencing increased interest in American farmhouse architecture. The nostalgia of returning to an earlier time and the appeal of a simpler, land-connected lifestyle are central to its renewed popularity. For some, the American farmhouse is perhaps the most tangible and sentimental connection to our country's rich history. It is an authentic, accessible and decidedly American artifact that holds a special place in our nation's architectural history.

While country farmhouse design

Wide floorboards and decorative hardware adds to the eighteenth-century feeling in the interior.

is a distinctly American aesthetic, it incorporates elements of country design from all over the world, including English cottage style and French country style. Also present in country farmhouse design are elements of Adirondack- and log cabin-style interior design. While these design styles may vary a great deal, the one common theme is the incorporation of the area's natural environment, such as woods, gardens, lakes, or the slope of the land to create a cozy, relaxed feel. The items you use in your country farmhouse-themed home may differ from the pieces used by someone in another part of the country because the design should be influenced by the natural elements in your area. Some basic things you can expect to find in country farmhouse design are:

- wooden floors covered with colorful throw rugs
- furniture covered in cotton or other natural fabrics (solid colors with homey throw pillows are popular, as is plaid fabric)
- antiqued metals
- floral patterns
- large pieces of furniture made of wood—usually a kind of wood that grows in the area

If there is one rule to country farmhouse design, it is accessorize, accessorize, accessorize! Knickknacks, pillows, wall art—these are the finishing touches that bring a country farmhouse home together. Look for things at the local flea market, show off your old family heirlooms, and by all means, display the artwork the kids create front and center. Don't worry about anything matching—in fact, the less matching there is, the more your home will have that charming, lived-in feel you're trying to create. Your home décor should evolve over time as you pick up more and more pieces to add to your rooms. In this instance, clutter is a virtue and will only add to the appeal of your country farmhouse-style décor.

A rustic farmhouse kitchen in a new house is modeled after farmhouses in the south of France. The new built-in oak cabinetry received a vintage look via artful distressing with bleach and wire brushing and was finished with green and taupe paints.

Victorian Style

The term Victorian architecture can refer to a number of architectural styles employed predominantly during the Victorian era. (The period of building that it covers, from 1837 to 1901, coincides with the actual reign of Queen Victoria, after whom it is named.) Victorian Gothic buildings feature arches, pointed windows, and other details borrowed from the Middle Ages; masonry Gothic revival buildings were often close replicas of medieval cathedrals. Wood-frame Gothic revival buildings often had lacy gingerbread trim and other playful details. If you like this style, newly manufactured gingerbread trim is sold at home centers and lumberyards, and it is easy to add to porch posts. As a rebellion against formal classical architecture, Italianate (Regency and early Victorian eras) became one of the most popular styles in the United States. With its low roofs, wide eaves, and ornamental brackets, Italianate is sometimes called the bracketed style.

A Victorian-style farmhouse in Maryland.

A stairway with turned mahogany balusters stands out against walls to which molding has been affixed to replicate panels and coffers.

The kitchen is light and bright and functional, with streamlined, contemporary appliances as well as painted furniture, mounted shelves, a chandelier, and simple cotton shades on the windows.

for muted tones, an appreciation for fine lines, and an inclination toward sparsely furnished rooms that renders their interiors quite sophisticated. They are also influenced by their surroundings, and a palette of sky blue and soft gray prevails. Painted floors are often adorned with a checkerboard or diamond pattern, most often in soft blue or gray and white. The Swedish home is usually devoid of clutter, but still has a very comfortable, lived-in feeling.

The Swedes understand the importance of light for well-being. In the dead of winter the sun doesn't come up until almost nine in the morning and sets six hours later, so they do everything possible to increase the amount of light in their homes. Windows, for example, are left undraped or, if privacy is an issue, covered with thin, gauzy drapes or muslin.

The bedroom is soft and calming in a pale blue and white palette.

Surfaces are painted light colors to reflect light, and blond woods such as birch, ash, and pine are popular. Fabrics are as pale in color as the painted walls. Lamps and candles are abundant, and mirrors or other glass objects are placed throughout a home to reflect their glow and enhance light.

SALVAGE SAVVY

Many owners of new houses use salvaged materials during the building process to give the rooms old-house character. These might include recycled floorboards, reclaimed and refitted barn doors, and pressed tin used to cover ceilings. Other homeowners incorporate salvaged materials into already built houses that lack the charming characteristics inherent in materials from the past.

Scandinavian Style

Another old-world style comes from Scandinavia. Pastel walls, homespun linens, and vintage fabrics capture the Scandinavian tradition; painted floors are typical. Comfort, beauty, and practicality define this style, and restraint is the secret to a well-designed home: the beauty is lost when there are too many details.

Take a cue from Scandinavian furnishings and consider a pale blue for a calming effect in the master bedroom. Keep all the bedding in this pale palette as well. Paint the floors white and leave them bare. Add a painted wooden bench in the room and soften it with a bevy of pillows covered in soft blue and white fabrics. Then introduce a side chair with a contrasting blue and white slipcover.

Small doses of red add a touch of punch to the overall blue and white scheme. Plates on the wall represent another Scandinavian decorating style.

A church window and pew capture the Scandinavian style.

You might cover the bedroom windows with simple Roman shades, which give you privacy when needed but also allow as much light into the rooms as possible. Use small touches of red as an accent color here and there. A mixture of carefully chosen textures and patterns will give each piece personality. Rugs are often checks or plaids in blue and white, as are curtain fabrics, upholstered furniture, and accessories.

The Swedes are devoted to wood, have a reverence for light, a preference

The Scandinavian tradition of painting floors defines and completes a room. The checkerboard pattern on the dining room floor is quite typical.

Red is another color typically found in Swedish homes. Here it is introduced sparingly in the living room.

There are many companies throughout the country that specialize in finding and selling salvaged goods. There are also contemporary artists and artisans who are continuing the American heritage of handcraftsmanship. These craftsmen and craftswomen are dedicated to faithfully reproducing Early American home furniture. They use antique lumber and traditional joinery that marks their work as handmade, and an aged finish that makes them appear as if they were a hundred years old.

Salvaged doors often come from farmhouses and barns that have been dismantled. For those homeowners who appreciate the intrinsic beauty and unique character of old wood, using reclaimed wood flooring is perfect. Planks re-milled from old railroad trestles, barns, and factories offer a distinctive option.

When laying new floors, some homeowners get an authentic aged look by using antique reproduction nails that replicate hand-forged nails from the eighteenth century. A black oxide finish makes them look like they were forged in a local blacksmith's shop. They have a square-cut, blunt-end design that allows them to pierce wood rather than slit it, for a more secure hold.

Other salvaged items used for new houses include leaded glass windows,

A vintage buffet, a staple in Swedish interiors, holds dinnerware.

farmhouse cabinets, stained glass, mantels, industrial lighting, iron gates, urns and garden ornaments, tiles, period lighting, lamp shades, mailboxes, historical bricks, sinks, and toilets. You'll find different items in different parts of the country.

The bedroom bench is softened with a group of pillows covered in pale blue and white printed fabrics.

Colonial Revival

Colonial homes are designed in the style of houses built by America's first European settlers—homes that were an imitation of English building styles of medieval times. The American Colonial style evolved in the early 1700s and was a manifestation of the imaginings and aspirations of these first colonists—and of their increasing prosperity. The traditional Colonial home consists of a two-story square or rectangular house with a steep, gabled roof; a large central door; a central chimney and fireplace; and an interior hallway off of which the home's rooms are found. This basic design has

Authentic touches abound in this kitchen, from rich brown cabinets to maple countertops. The "cage bar" (the tall cupboard on the left) is a special addition, used in early inns and taverns to lock away the liquor.

The homeowners enclosed the staircase in painted bead board paneling and dropped the 16-foot ceiling to 8 feet.

Blue shutters on a Cape-style house built in 1988 were painted Colonial red, and a split-rail fence was added to give it the look of an eighteenth-century farmhouse.

Above left: Blacksmith-forged iron hinges add period-appropriate touches.

Above Right: Painted 16- to 18-inch wide-board paneling was used to help hide sheetrock in order to mimic eighteenth-century styles.

served as the jumping-off point for a number of other house designs that continue to be popular today.

With a minimal investment, a little paint, some hard work, and a creative imagination, you can transform your ordinary house into a historic-looking house more reflective of the style and time period you love. One couple began with a 16-foot ceiling and open foyer that was particularly out of place in their vision of an Early American home. So they enclosed the staircase with paneled bead board and dropped the front hall ceiling to 8 feet. Additional renovation included replacing laminate countertops with maple and substituting vinyl floors with wood that was painted with two layers of color—Spanish brown and harvest gold—so the darker color would wear through over time. On their own, the homeowners were able to remove wallpaper and carpeting from a bedroom, as well as add corner beams and wide-plank pine floors, replace doors, and install window casings with 4-inch moldings throughout the house.

Bungalow Style

Bungalows, cottages, and cabins are thought of as vacation homes, usually small in size and rustic in décor. Many of these houses were built by a lake, in the mountains, in the woods, or at the seashore. Simple in design, their furnishings are meant to promote carefree living and maintenance-free upkeep. Hooks and shelves positioned for easy use, for example, may substitute for closets and dressers. Towels and baseball hats can hang from pegs, ready for a day at the beach. New hardware and a coat of white paint might be the only things needed to upgrade a charming rustic kitchen.

Bungalow style is as much a state of mind as a destination. Such homes are a real retreat, places where a family can relax and enjoy a simple way of living, like a beach cottage filled with collections gathered from childhood walks along the seashore. Furnishings should reflect a personal vision of the perfect getaway.

Gather natural materials from your surroundings—pine cones and needles for sachets and stuffed pillows, or sea glass and seashells to display on windowsills; a vacation home can be accessorized entirely with these finds.

A 1950s-era bungalow becomes a little cottage for family retreats. The Adirondack chairs and hydrangea bushes give it a relaxed, summery feeling.

Mix the things you love, adding shelves wherever needed, and rearrange every time you get the urge. Out of sight can mean out of mind, so display dishes artfully on open shelves, where they are always visible and ready to be used.

Built in 1927, every square inch of this tiny bungalow is decorated with flea market and antique store finds that reflect the period of the house.

2

AGING YOUR NEW HOME

Good design borrowed from the past adds character to any house. Even if your home is contemporary, you can begin a step-by-step "backdating" with a bit of creativity and ingenuity, transforming your home with a select mix of architectural materials, antiques, and thrift shop treasures.

The easiest and most affordable way to age your new home is with paint—on walls, furniture, and floors. Weathered, painted furniture in shades of white and neutral blends easily into a contemporary setting and is quintessential vintage revival; choosing colors from Colonial times will instantly transform your rooms from new to old. Floors treated with a painted checkerboard pattern and stenciled walls are other old-house features.

Another way to introduce old-world character into each room is with details and finishing touches such as molding around windows and doors and bead board on kitchen or bathroom walls. For a minimal investment, you can replace new doorknobs and hinges and substitute wide moldings for window casings. Wide-plank pine floors were often found in early homes as well. Fireplace mantels and surrounds made from salvaged wood give a room that certain character, as do reproduction rough-hewn beams (or authentic ones, if you can find them) for a ceiling or as open shelves in a kitchen. Characterless rooms can be transformed by installing painted wide-board paneling over sheetrock and using pine floors rather than traditional hardwood or carpeting.

The living room has been masterfully re-created to incorporate period furniture and details that were often found in eighteenth-century homes. Metal hinges on doors, exposed ceiling beams, a wide-board fireplace surround, pine floors, wingback chairs, and shelves holding early containers makes one want to ask, "Is that old or new?"

Redefining spaces and reusing, recycling, and renewing materials may be just what a house needs to banish its new-house look. And the process needn't be complicated. One homeowner moved a refrigerator in her kitchen to an adjacent laundry room, then fitted its remaining niche with shelves to form a shallow pantry. (Pantries were often found in old houses but rarely make an appearance in new homes.) An arched screen door that she found subsequently became the door front for the pantry. Another homeowner installed an old window that she found at a garage sale in a sunroom and then lined the ceiling with old wooden doors to add geometry and the warmth of painted wood. A porcelain sink and cabinets with peeling paint are often more appealing for their charm and quaintness than a kitchen that is streamlined and modern. Metal scraps are favorite salvaged items as well. Columns with peeling paint are often used as decorative elements, lending visual interest, if not practicality, to a room.

Sometimes the design of a house comes about in a most unexpected way. You might be visiting a historic village or on a house and garden tour in your area, or stumble upon a store that sells early furniture. Something about the muted colors, simple forms, and rich history of Pilgrim or William and Mary furniture speaks to you. The next thing you know, you are designing your house to reflect the simple grace of another time.

Remember that rooms in a house do not have to be used as originally intended.

A reclaimed fireplace mantle provides the framework for a painting and a pile of vintage fabrics.

PAINT

There are two attitudes toward historic paint colors. One is to reproduce the color exactly the way it was used two hundred years ago, when the colors were often much brighter than people expect. Bold colors on walls and furnishings allowed rural homemakers to brighten their surroundings in centuries past, and colors such as red, blue, and mustard give an instant 1800s look to a room. The other technique is to make colors look like they have been around for two hundred years. This ages a room immediately.

When choosing colors for your rooms, pick a palette and stick with it. For example, you might paint the walls, crown moldings, baseboards, and built-ins in one color, such as Benjamin Moore's Westminster Gold #200, a historic color that would be good in a family room. The mix of high-gloss and satin finishes promotes a feeling of depth.

For a vintage look use two or three strong colors and repeat them in fabrics, walls, art, and accessories; furniture is either upholstered in vivid fabric or given a coat of bold paint. The consistent color scheme will allow you to harmoniously mix old and new, high and low.

TIPS FOR USING COLOR

1. Keep color simple—limit yourself to two or three colors in each room. This will allow you to create an eclectic mix without the room appearing overly busy.
2. Lighten floors. Painting floorboards white is an inexpensive way to make a house look fresh and up-to-date.
3. Hang pictures of similar theme or subject in even-numbered groups in same-color frames to make a strong statement. This also helps maintain overall visual balance.

Green (on the walls) and red (on the shutters) are used to brighten rural farmhouses.

This bedroom features walls painted in a subtle whitewash and a tin ceiling reclaimed from a New Orleans opera house.

PAINT TECHNIQUES

In order to make new kitchen cabinets look old, consider the technique of distressing: Gently weather the cabinets with bleach and wire brushing, then finish them with a rub of green and taupe paints. Aging new doors with the help of a faux painting technique is easy. Apply Ralph Lauren's Tobacco glaze atop a base coat of warm bisque paint to create an aged patina.

A fresco-like finish can be created by mixing paint with plaster. Try Ralph Lauren Ballroom Gold metallic latex paint for the walls and Ralph Lauren Big Sky latex paint for the ceiling. For an aged patina, prime a piece of furniture with Zinsser Bulls Eye 1-2-3. It sticks to anything without having to sand. Then brush on Benjamin Moore Deep Poinsettia in eggshell-finish latex. Next, apply a

The weathered blue paint on a chest of drawers found in an antique shop is a typical color used on furniture in early homes.

crackling medium, allowing it to dry, and then paint on a coat of Benjamin Moore White Dove pearl-finish latex.

Sponge painting was a technique often used in older homes to give walls texture. It is easy to do with two paint colors and a natural sponge. Begin by painting the walls with one color. When dry, dip the natural sponge into a contrasting paint color. Next, tap the sponge onto newsprint to remove excess paint and, using a light touch, "pounce" the color onto the painted walls to create a cloudlike texture. Continue to do this until you have created a soft, subtle, overall pattern.

The fresco-like finish was applied to the ceiling of a bathroom.

CHECKERBOARD FLOORS

In Colonial times, floors were often treated with a painted checkerboard pattern in bold, contrasting colors. This characteristic of early decoration can, however, be reinterpreted for modern times: A combination of soft green and cream hues is reminiscent of the past while being fresh and up-to-date.

Wide-plank floors, especially in the kitchen, lend themselves to a

checkerboard paint application. The first thing to do is decide on a design. Do you want a border? Where do you want the design to begin? Should it be overall, or just in the center of the room to look like an area rug? Sketch it out and play with the proportions.

A wide-plank kitchen floor is painted in a checkerboard design of soft green and ivory colors. The same green is used on the kitchen table and pantry walls.

An old claw-foot tub was painted and stenciled. The floor is painted with a checkerboard pattern and the walls are bead board, in keeping with the Early American cottage style.

The checkerboard floor is a soft green and cream, imitating the paint technique often used in old houses.

AGING YOUR NEW HOME 59

WOOD FLOORING

Variegated wide-plank flooring with a distressed finish is a classic country look and can become an essential element in a room. It's possible to find salvaged flooring, but you can also buy new flooring that has been produced to look old.

Oak floors that are stained or painted a dark color—a refreshing take on early floor treatments—make a dramatic statement for an all-white or pastel environment. Over time, a patina will develop from the wear and tear on the floors.

Dark oak floors make bright white furnishings pop.

Nothing brings warmth and natural beauty to a room like a hardwood floor.

STENCILED WALLS

In the eighteenth and nineteenth centuries, stencils were often used on walls to simulate expensive wallpaper, printed or embroidered textiles, and woven rugs. This stenciling was usually done by traveling artisans who went from one job to the next with their collection of stencil patterns, dry pigments, and stubby brushes. Early wallpaper patterns were simplified and enlarged, making them more practical (and more economical) than small, all-over patterns. A simple border at the top of the wall often replaced fancier molding around a room. Wall stenciling reached its greatest popularity in the Federal period, from 1783 to the 1820s. At that time, it was fashionable to define the outlines or edges of patterns and shapes.

For a while in the 1800s, it was very popular for young ladies at boarding schools to learn the art and craft of theorem painting. This special type of stencil work was usually done on velvet. The patterns, typically fruit or flowers, were carefully arranged to make a skillfully shaded still-life "painting" that was framed and often hung in a parlor. The use of metallic powders for stenciling also became popular in the nineteenth century. Elaborate designs in faux gold and silver imitated the expensive inlaid metals and Oriental lacquer that were much admired and collected at the time. Later in the nineteenth century, stencil designs were used to apply decoration to furniture in factories like the Hitchcock Chair Factory in Connecticut.

Stenciling Today

A part of America's colorful past, stenciling is an easy technique to learn—providing an accessible way to add old-world charm to your new rooms. While early stencils were usually made of heavy oiled paper and later made of tin and specially treated

An Early American stencil design is applied to a hallway wall to give it old-world charm.

Folk murals such as the one on this wall were typically painted by nineteenth-century itinerant folk artists. Two local artisans created the mural for this house.

linen, the most common modern stencil material is strong, flexible plastic. A multicolor pattern usually requires a separate stencil for each color (three colors, three stencils). Early stencil designs have been reproduced and are available in fine art stores.

Today, stencilers rarely use oil-based paint, instead working with fast-drying acrylics that reduce smudging and speed up the work. Until after the Civil War, most painters made their own paints by mixing the chosen medium with dry pigments. Typical pre-1850 colors were black, yellow ochre, red ochre, and (after 1704) Prussian blue. The colors used for Early American stencil designs were usually very strong; because houses were dark and cold, people wanted to introduce brightness through color. Benjamin Moore sells a line of small bottles of historic latex paint colors that are perfect for stenciling an early design with modern-day ease.

FLOORCLOTH

Canvas floorcloths were used to cover the floors in many eighteenth-century homes. Floorcloths date from fourteenth-century France but reached their height in popularity in the 1600s in England, where they usually replicated the look of expensive marble tile. The settlers of America brought the technique across the ocean, using the cloths to insulate, protect, and enliven the floors in their New World homes. These floor coverings have always been constructed from canvas sailcloth, made impervious by the application of oil-based paints.

The earliest floorcloths were the simplest, most often displaying a tile or woodlike design. Later, natural motifs emerged. As time progressed, the range of colors used expanded from black, red, and white to a range of saturated hues including Prussian blue, malachite, and ochre. Many artisans used stencils to repeat a regular pattern over a large area. (The same stencils were often used on walls.)

Early American homes often used stenciled, canvas floorcloths to cover floors.

HOW TO MAKE A FLOORCLOTH

Size both sides of a sailcloth with two coats of oil-based primer to prevent shrinking.

1. Fold a one-inch border around the entire sailcloth, miter the corners, and bind with hide glue.
2. Apply three coats of the base color, using oil-based paints such as those from Old Village.
3. Draw and color the pattern freehand or using a stencil.
4. Apply eight coats of polyurethane to seal the design.

PERIOD-STYLE WALLPAPERS

Add depth to your walls with high-quality papers that feature historic patterns and are made with historic techniques. York, the oldest manufacturer in the United States, based the papers in its Mount Vernon collection on textiles, wallpapers, and journals contained in the archives of George Washington's famous Virginia estate. (For more information, visit www.yorkwall.com).

Farrow & Ball (www.farrow-ball.com) creates its Silvergate papers using patterns and block-printing techniques from the nineteenth century. But modern water-based colors make these replicas stain resistant, washable, and low in volatile organic compounds.

Many of the patterns in the Brewster Wallcovering Company's new vintage Heritage collection include toile, damask, and florals. These are surface printed, a nineteenth-century process that lays down copious amounts of ink to yield a handcrafted look (www.brewsterwallcovering.com).

The artisans at Adelphi Paper Hangings (www.adelphipaperhangings.com) employ methods used by craftspeople from the 1720s to the 1860s to reproduce wallpapers. William Morris' designs from the Arts and Crafts period are available in historically accurate colors made from natural dyes like madder and indigo.

Don't overlook the ceiling. A medallion-patterned wallpaper from Farrow & Ball, for example, might support a room's overall color scheme and add visual interest to the ceiling. It makes a room appear larger but still cozy.

TRIM WORK

Trim work is one of the most important decorative elements in a home, providing a level of texture and depth that creates mood and style. Historically, trim evolved alongside architectural styles, so it's important to match moldings to the style and spirit of the era that you want your home to emulate. When done correctly, trim work lends polish, detail, and authenticity to your home. Trim can also help differentiate rooms. More ornate, layered looks are common in public areas, while private rooms, such as bedrooms, have less elaborate moldings.

Wood and plaster are preferred for their authenticity, but lightweight polyurethane is lower maintenance and much easier for the do-it-yourselfer to install; there are many such trims made to look like the originals.

Ceiling medallions allow you to echo the decorative elements in a room.

Add moldings to create an interesting fireplace surround.

Consider the proportions of the room when choosing a size and whether you will need to drill an opening for light fixtures.

When it comes to fireplace mantels, designs run the gamut from stark to ornate. When built up with decorative moldings, the mantel becomes a sculptural element. Consider adding some of these moldings to give your fireplace a more interesting profile.

A pediment from the doorway of an old house hangs over the living room window, while elements salvaged from a church flank each side.

Reproductions of early ceiling medallions can be found in home centers and lumberyards.

Opposite Page: A piece of decorative trim divides the living room from the dining space behind it. A pale palette imbues the home with romantic old world charm.

Left: A dreary old fireplace was replaced by a vintage mantel that the owner inlaid with shards of antique china. White mirrors are layered against the mirrored wall over the fireplace, and white pitchers in different heights and sizes are filled with white flowers for a romantic display.

Below: Oversize antique library display cases were found at an auction and now show off a collection of ivory-colored china against a background of sea glass. The table was made from an old barn door topped with glass and set on porch posts from Home Depot.

SALVAGE SAVVY

Almost anything from the past can be reinvented for a purpose different from its original one. A piece of gingerbread trim from an old house, for example, might become a visual room divider, separating living and dining areas.

While original pieces of old house interiors are available from salvage and restoration companies, it's easier to find newly reproduced architectural details to use as decorative elements in your new home. Finely crafted cornice and crown moldings, ceiling centers and domes, pilaster capitals, wall niches, fireplace mantels, chair rails, door casings, and brackets are just some of the products available at home centers; most are easy to install without professional help.

Old doors and doorknobs create instant aging for a new house.

ANTIQUE TIEBACKS

Finishing touches such as antique tassel tiebacks quickly and easily lend character to new draperies. Tassel tiebacks from the seventeenth through the nineteenth centuries were always meant to bring a little bit of drama to an interior, and even today these delicate textiles are being employed for a bit of panache. They add a wonderful, opulent look to simple draperies and can even serve as art objects, contributing something quite special to a room.

In well-proportioned seventeenth-century European homes, tassels were applied to the corners of pillows, bed hangings, and draperies. In the nineteenth century, tassels were attached to braided silk, wool, or linen ropes to create formal curtain tiebacks.

Tassel tie-backs were hand woven by expert tassel and braid makers. Tassels as small as 1 inch to as large as 10 inches were then attached to ropes. Hand-dyed

Doorplates and hinges complement antique doorknobs.

Antique tassel tiebacks add an old-world touch to new draperies.

examples can be found in rich, bold hues of gold, blue, red, and yellow. A vintage tieback can range from forty to six hundred dollars, depending on its condition and the intricacy of the tassel and braid.

ANTIQUE DOORKNOBS

Antique doorknobs—another finishing touch—lend subtle character to a room. They can be used on room or closet doors but also make an interesting collection when displayed in an attractive way. They can be found at salvage stores, antiques shops, and online auctions. Before you buy, make sure all of the parts are intact and in good condition, and will fit the

ANATOMY OF A DOORKNOB

Spindle: Most antique doorknobs come in pairs, screwed onto either end of a long rod or square spindle. If the spindle is missing, replacements can be found in hardware stores.

Base: Knob bases are often set into rosettes or circular plates that can be unadorned or ornamental.

Knob: Material affects desirability. Clear glass, porcelain, and decorative brass are fairly easy to find. Clear glass is the most common, while blue, green, red, and amber glass are harder to find and therefore more expensive.

Antique doorknobs range from simple to elaborate.

door you have in mind. Those that are well designed but lack the working mechanism are perfect for a display and will cost less. (A good source of leads is www.antiquedoorknobs.org.)

LIGHTING

Use early or reproduction lighting fixtures as a way to add some old-fashioned appeal to your rooms. Crystal and wrought iron chandeliers, indoor and outdoor lanterns, and candlestick lights are just a few of the myriad of lighting options. When choosing fixtures, try to find at least one that makes a statement with a distinctive detail. If it's an antique, make sure the wiring is sound before installing it. Find lamps at antique shops and then add a colorful new shade. Remember that recessed ceiling lights look new; table lamps offer more options. An alternative to recessed lighting in a kitchen might be reproduction European pulley lights or a chandelier—or even two.

Reproduction lighting fixtures are comprised of three components: design, construction, and finish. Many companies offer fixtures that are faithful reproductions. Through special techniques, the various finishes are made to appear exactly like an original, indistinguishable from antiques two hundred years old or even older.

The light fixture in the dining room once hung in an old elevator.

Candlestick light fixtures like this chandelier are in keeping with the eighteenth-century spirit of this house.

PLACEMENT POINTERS

The Right Height: Most people hang chandeliers too high. A general rule of thumb is to hang the fixture so that the bottom of the chandelier is between 27 and 36 inches above the tabletop.

The Right Size: The dining room is the perfect place to let your chandelier make a statement. When in doubt, think big, especially if you have high ceilings.

The Right Shape: Let your furnishings guide your lighting purchases. Relate the shape to your dining table and chairs. If the table is round, the fixture should be, too.

What Wattage? For the most pleasing atmosphere and overall effect, try a fixture with many sources of lower-wattage bulbs—an eight-arm chandelier with 40-watt bulbs, for instance. And always install a dimmer switch.

Look for lamps and candelabras made from old lamp parts. Always have a professional install hardwired lighting fixtures.

A medley of European pulley lights is a good alternative to recessed lighting in a kitchen.

RETRO KITCHENS

The appliances in the kitchen are modern, but everything else is salvaged and has had another life. Cabinets are from the 1920s and topped with marble or stainless steel. The work island is an enamel-topped table.

The best thing about a new house is that the kitchen and bathrooms are new, with fixtures and plumbing that work perfectly. Unfortunately, these very things are often at odds with the old-house charm you are trying to achieve. Many homeowners do not want to sacrifice the convenience of modern appliances and opt for stainless steel, but then conceal them by covering them in a vintage guise of treated wood (which can also be used on the fronts of cabinets). Many appliance companies are

reproducing appliances from the 1930s and 1940s; Magic Chef, for example, makes a wonderful vintage oven as part of its 1000 Series.

A retro kitchen never goes out of style. To create your own, begin by considering the paint color for the walls. Retro shades include mint green, cream, yellow, pale blue, and pink—all the colors found in

Open shelves on iron brackets painted to match the mirror are practical and good-looking. The 1940s refrigerator and deep porcelain sink came from an estate sale.

Large casement windows, white cabinets, a tiled backsplash, an open-beamed ceiling, and a bead board paneled island add to the farmhouse-style kitchen.

Fiestaware, a popular and colorful line of everyday pottery from the 1930s. Next, consider painting the floors. A checkerboard treatment was often found in older homes.

Bead board cabinetry is reminiscent of early country homes and is often used in new kitchens to conceal appliances and cover walls; it is also popular for the bathroom. Pine kitchen tables, rather than islands, were staples in Early American homes across the country. Another

feature found in early kitchens is open storage. Simple shelving make dishes easy to get at; consider vintage brackets for the shelves. A vertical plate rack attached to the wall is another useful way to store plates as they did in the past.

Many homeowners are attracted to anything old, worn, peeling, and "dirty." They look for creative alternative materials for conventional cupboards and counters. For example, shelves from a restaurant supply store might hold

A refrigerator is covered with distressed wood to blend in seamlessly with the twin pantries on either side.

The kitchen eschews sleek modernity, opting for charm and a retro look. Pale green is the color of choice, from the cabinets (one houses the dishwasher) to the dishtowels. A vintage tablecloth hides plumbing under the porcelain sink.

Appliances are concealed in vintage guise. The cabinet to the right of the sink was built deeper than normal to conceal the dishwasher and microwave. All the furniture in this room is reproduction and a good illustration of how style and convenience can coexist.

canisters and coffee mugs or teacups. Glass-front cabinets can be given a dose of vintage charm with lacy organza napkins tacked inside the panes. A vintage tablecloth might be turned into a "skirt" to hide unsightly plumbing and storage underneath a sink, for an inexpensive and quick touch of ephemera.

It's easy to add accessories to a kitchen, whether they are the real things or reproductions. Not everything need be old, but it is good to mix a few authentic pieces with the copies so no one will be the wiser. Discount outlets offer copies of retro kitchen accessories such as small mixers, colanders, breadboxes, canisters, dishtowels, and chinaware in pastel colors and vintage patterns. Hunt yard sales and flea markets for items that appear retro but simply need a coat of paint, such as kitchen chairs and tables. They don't have to match. In fact, the charm is in the mixing of colors and shapes.

FIESTAWARE

Fiestaware, the colorful pottery for everyday use, was developed by Frederick Hurten Rhead during the mid-1930s for the Homer Laughlin Pottery Company in Newell, West Virginia. In 1935 he created the ware that became the company's most popular and most collected line in red, cobalt, light green, yellow, and ivory. Turquoise came along slightly later. Rhead's Fiesta would continue to be produced for almost twenty-five years until it was restyled in 1959 and replaced with Fiesta Ironstone, which was discontinued in 1973. Peak production for the company was in 1948, when the company produced 10,129,449 dishes.

Reproduction beams, blue/green paint, and vintage cabinet pulls stocked with Fiestaware dishes are details used to age a new kitchen

RETRO BATHROOMS

Classic claw-foot tubs are easy to find and add a retro style to your new bathroom. Most cast-iron tubs have a plain white finish, but painting the exterior to match your bathroom can add a splash of color.

Retro bathrooms are easy to create with vintage elements. For example, painted white pressed tin can be used on walls or the ceiling for a period-appropriate alternative to traditional tiles or bead board. In place of modern lighting, early chandeliers add elegance. Salvaged tubs have real vintage appeal. Because the plumbing for claw-foot models typically comes up through the floor, consult a professional plumber about retrofitting your bathroom. Classic claw-foot tubs—new or old—are available in sizes from 4 to 6 feet long and are easy to find.

Cast-iron reproduction tubs look authentically old-fashioned, and you can usually paint the exterior to match your bathroom's décor. Expect prices to run up to several thousand dollars. Because cast iron tubs can weigh nearly 1,000 pounds when filled with water, consult a contractor experienced in installing this type of tub before you buy to ensure that your floor can support the weight.

Acrylic tubs are much lighter than their cast-iron counterparts, and better insulators. American Bath Factory's models come with hardware and cost around fifteen hundred dollars at Lowe's stores.

Complete your vintage tub with a retro-style shower curtain easily made from a chenille bedspread. Hem it to the proper length and install sturdy rivets to hold the shower hooks. Circular shower rods are available from renovation supply houses.

Early homes did not have built-in cabinetry in the bathroom. Storage might be housed in an armoire or a painted wall cabinet. A large pedestal sink with an oversize mirror in a vintage frame will give the impression of a vanity.

This bathroom is outfitted entirely with vintage elements: painted pressed tin walls, a reenameled vintage tub, and an early 1900s French chandelier.

| 3 |

FURNITURE

It's not necessary to find expensive, authentic antiques to furnish the rooms of your house. There are many well-designed and reasonably priced reproduction furniture pieces and accessories to be found, as well as innovative ways to arrange things to create the look of an early home. Often one cannot tell the difference between an old or reproduction piece, especially when the new pieces are mixed with early accessories and collections.

It's easy to create old-world charm with furniture, paint, and accessories. Paint manufacturers, such as Benjamin Moore and Sherwin Williams, have come out with extensive lines of Colonial paint colors that are perfectly matched to those found in early American homes. Paint is an easy, inexpensive way to give

your rooms character and also a good way to transform reproduction and unfinished furniture.

How do you begin? It's a good idea to buy the largest pieces first in order to anchor the room. These might include a cupboard, a sideboard, or a sofa. You might buy antique wooden pieces and new upholstered furniture, such as the sofa and chairs for the living room. Once you have a plan for what you will need you can add the smaller pieces, mixing old and new based on what you can afford, what you might have inherited or already own, and what you find. While some people take great satisfaction from planning their entire house, researching and buying the furnishings all at once, most find it more satisfying—and often

A pediment from the doorway of an old house hangs over the living room window, while elements salvaged from a church flank each side.

With limited kitchen space, architectural elements are layered upward on walls and atop cabinets. The work island is an old store counter.

An oil portrait of undisclosed origin hangs above an early nineteenth-century jelly cupboard. An antique European wooden bowl holds pears, and hog-scraper candlesticks complete this simple arrangement.

Illustrated portraits found on eBay are tacked to the wall of the bedroom. A mix of blue and white prints, stripes, ticking, and patchwork make an iron bed look cozy and inviting.

more practical—to buy one piece at a time or to furnish one room at a time.

As you add furniture, live with each new piece for a while. Get used to it in the space and then get a feeling for the next thing you might need. Rearranging, editing, exchanging, and selectively choosing new pieces to throw into the mix is an ongoing challenge that can be compelling and an interesting way to live. Many homeowners enjoy the process of decorating their homes so much that they have made it into a lifelong hobby, one that they admit will probably never end. They enjoy perfecting their homes, and doing so gives meaning to travel and leisure time. Even if you are unsure about how to put things together, once you get started it will not take long to become confident about marrying pieces from different styles and periods with contemporary reproductions.

An actual front porch with mail still in the mailbox, from a house in Louisville, Kentucky, now graces the sunroom.

MIXING OLD AND NEW FURNITURE

If you are in love with antique furniture but can't always find exactly what you want or can't afford the things you love, look for reproductions that are faithful to nineteenth-century favorites. As a rule, reproduction furniture, such as a chest of drawers, functions better than the original, but mixing in a genuine antique, such as a blanket chest or night table, helps root the reproductions in authenticity.

Most homeowners opt to buy upholstered sofas and chairs that are new, surrounding them with early wooden pieces. However, vintage upholstered

In the old days, linen tea towels were monogrammed with hand-embroidered stitches. If you find them, it isn't important that the monogram be personal. They add a vintage touch to any kitchen or bathroom.

A sunroom evokes another time. Painted antiques like the 1920s American writing desk and Louis XVI–style chair, a collage of sepia photographs, and an assortment of ephemera are carefully arranged as if they had always been there.

Sugar and flour canisters from the 1920s were flea market finds. Today it is possible to find reproductions that look quite authentic.

furniture is very affordable and can be easily found at flea markets and yard sales. If necessary these pieces can be rebuilt, restuffed, and reupholstered to create an interesting mélange of vintage-style furniture.

Carefully mixing reproduction furniture with original antiques makes it hard to distinguish between the two. As long as the new pieces with which you furnish your rooms have the right look, combining antiques with reproductions will make your house feel old. For example, a mid-nineteenth-century rope bed covered with a Victorian crazy-

GRANDFATHER CLOCKS

The grandfather clock has become one of those sought-after antiques that lends respectability and quality to a home. Grandfather clocks originated in the late 1600s in London. Owning a tall clock, as it was first known in the United States, conveyed status. In the 1880s, America named the clock "grandfather" after a popular song about a clock that stopped when its ninety-year-old owner died. Perhaps, like any respected head of a household, the grandfather—whether the man or the piece of furniture—carries a certain air of worldliness, presiding over his domain and making everyone feel just a little more secure.

quilt bedspread in a guest room might be paired with what looks like an early primitive hooked rug on the wall. Many modern manufacturers are reproducing designs found in early hooked rugs at very reasonable prices. Because the designs are authentic and the wool is the same type that was used to hook the originals, it will be very difficult for anyone but a collector or a dealer to perceive the difference.

The original farmhouse sink, faucet, and tiles reinforce the kitchen's vintage feel.

You might place a new grandfather clock in a hallway next to a circa 1800s Windsor chair. A newly crafted sideboard might be painted Colonial red and hold a display that includes pewter candlesticks and a wooden firkin on an early wooden tray. Collections that are true to their origin are full of character—and don't cost a lot of money.

Attention to detail makes any house interesting. To that end, furnishings and accessories should be well planned—and meant to be used. Everything can be aesthetically pleasing but utilitarian at the same time. In this way you can enjoy living with things that have stood the test of time along with the newer pieces that are reminiscent of an earlier period.

An English chaise provides a cozy retreat within a retreat. The dog portrait was purchased at a flea market.

CUPBOARDS

Most Colonial homes counted at least one cupboard among its furnishings. Corner and open cupboards were used to store china, glassware, pewter, linens, quilts, and other household furnishings. They were almost always painted, as they were often made of inferior woods. Cupboards serve the same utilitarian purpose in households today, but they also provide a fine background for displaying collections and make a dramatic decorating statement. A corner cupboard anchors and creates a focal point in any room.

In the parlor, a nineteenth-century step-back cupboard is paired with reproduction furnishings.

ARMOIRES

Older homes were traditionally sparse on closets. (One of the advantages of a new home is closet space, although some homeowners never seem to have enough!) Years ago families either didn't own so many clothes, or they solved the problem with armoires.

Armoires are pieces of rather large-size furniture that often dominated bedrooms. They are a necessary prop in period comedic movies, in which there always seems to be a lover hiding in a

An old side board and iron bed dominate the bedroom. Painted wall treatment is reminiscent of early homes.

carved wooden armoire beneath billowing petticoats when his mistress' husband appears on the scene. Descendants of medieval storage cabinets used for armor (hence the name), armoires stored clothes or linens in bedrooms centuries ago. Like most things that are made well, the armoire has survived, although its appearance has changed a bit to accommodate modern needs. A lovely old armoire can become the focal point of a room and serve all sorts of practical uses. Its uses are limited only by imagination, especially because rooms increasingly tend to serve more than one purpose.

Sources of Reproduction Armoires

The Borkholder Corporation (www. borkholder.com), a furniture maker in the Amish country of Napanee, Indiana, offers reproduction armoires in oak and cherry. Its best seller is patterned after an old German design with simple lines and arched trim. "The cherry wood it is made of is simply oiled so that it has a natural look with a burnt-orange flavor," says Dwayne Borkholder, whose Amish-born father owns the company. "The beauty of the cherry is that the more it ages, the more character it takes on, and the deeper the grain looks," he adds. "You get a much richer appearance as time goes on."

The four-poster bed is a reproduction and a good example of how easily a new piece can be paired with antiques—a love seat and coverlet circa 1885.

in a bedroom was flipped, and the unscarred undersides of the boards were whitewashed.

When buying an armoire keep this in mind: Bigger may be better in the large rooms of today's homes, but make sure you can actually get a piece into place. Armoires can be difficult to move into upstairs bedrooms, for example. A lot of people fall in love with a piece but find they cannot get it into their homes. Fortunately, some models can be dismantled and reassembled to make moving them easier.

There are also many companies that specialize in reproduction armoires based on French models built in the 1700s. Thomasville, for example, has models that include Spanish and French designs in maple and oak, with ornate carving and raised panels.

A well-made, interesting piece of furniture that has been copied from the past always lends character to a room; this particular piece is practical as well. Armoires are often used to hide Sub-Zero refrigerators and freezers that seem out of place in a kitchen retrofitted with cabinets made of reclaimed wood.

Opposite Page: Mustard yellow is a typical Colonial paint color. Shuttered windows and pine boards covering the wall up to the wainscoting are details found in early houses.

Left: Give wood floors an authentic aged look with antique reproduction nails that replicate hand-forged nails from the eighteenth century.

PAINTED COUNTRY FURNITURE

Antique country furniture—utilitarian pieces like kitchen tables, chairs, and cabinets—was handcrafted by rural furniture makers. It was painted for several reasons. An assortment of poor-quality woods was often used. Paint hid a multitude of sins: knots, coarse grain, and the fact that several types of wood might be used on a single piece. Paint also protected the wood. Some original painted pieces were adorned with illustrations or stencil designs. They lend a charming,

informal country feeling to any contemporary home.

You may discover separate pieces of furniture that can be put together to make one interesting piece. For example, it's easy to paint a dresser and a mirror with a base in a color that ties the two pieces together. By placing the mirror and base on top of the dresser, you will create one important and dramatic object that can become the focal point of the room. Consider also painting a few accessories in the same (or a contrasting) color to put on the dresser. Unfinished furniture with characteristic vintage lines offers another option for creating the look of early painted furniture without the expense—and the time it takes to hunt for exactly what you need. Then paint or stain the piece to make it look old (see sidebar on page 101). Antiquing kits for creating instant aging on any wooden piece of furniture are also sold in paint and hardware stores.

What if you find a piece of furniture that is literally falling apart? First determine if any part of it is salvageable. For example, if you find an old painted dresser that is beyond repair, look at the individual drawers to see if the drawer fronts can be preserved for hanging on the wall as art. A drawer front, or two together, might even have potential as

A silver server would be right at home in an English country cottage at tea time. A lace runner and pastel still life complete the vignette.

White Meakin china purchased on eBay fills a pine hutch. Ivory lace edging lends a European flair to the shelves, and a chandelier adds a romantic touch over the table.

A rickety bench is not stable enough for sitting but provides an interesting object over which to drape blankets at the end of a bed. Iron bed frames are good vintage items and look especially wonderful when covered with a lace coverlet or even a tablecloth combined with lots of shabby-chic pillows.

a headboard for a bed. Another might be hung on the wall, and its knobs used for hanging clothes. A drawer front might have potential as a towel holder in the bathroom, and yet another as the background for mounting a narrow mirror. If the paint is peeling away in an interesting way, there is always a way to find another use for such an item.

How to Tell an Antique from a Reproduction

How can you tell if a piece is old? A painted antique chair will show increased signs of wear at the ends of the arms, where the hands would naturally rest and rub off the paint more than underneath the arm. If the wear is consistent through the piece, it's likely a reproduction that has been distressed to appear old.

Because no one would see them, it simply made no sense to furniture makers to paint the insides of drawers or the bottoms of tables: They didn't feel it was necessary to waste the time and paint. The insides of drawers, chair bottoms, and the like will, however, be painted on reproductions.

New furniture is painted with water-based acrylics that were invented in the 1940s. Old furniture will be painted with milk- or oil-based paints. Old paint is very hard and breaks off into irregular pieces because it is very brittle. If you try to scrape it off with a knife, it will come off in jagged pieces. New paint is soft. When scraped with a knife, it will come off in curls.

HOW TO DISTRESS CABINETS

Here's how to make a newly purchased piece of furniture look old:

1. Use medium to fine (80 to 200-grit) sandpaper to sand down the finish on your piece so the primer and paint has something to which to adhere.
2. Take a few tools (a hammer, screwdriver, chain, set of keys, etc.) and rough up its surface. Faux "worm holes" can be created with a small wire nail and a hammer. A wire brush and a sand block add more character.
3. Use a good-quality white primer and give the wood a thin coat. After the primer has dried, follow up with a light sanding. Apply a top coat in the desired color and while it's still wet, rub some of the paint off.
4. Another way to get an aged-looking patina is by rubbing the distressed wood with two different gel stain colors. Use a rag, alternating the colors in about 12-inch irregular patches. Gel stain dries slowly, so you can work with it until you create the look you like. You'll get the hang of this technique pretty quickly—just glop on the gel stain with one rag (or a sponge brush) and then wipe it off with another. Try to clean more off in some places and leave some spots darker. Leave plenty of stain in the nooks and crannies to accentuate the worn areas and bring out any details, especially on furniture.

Vintage textiles bring a lived-in element to any room and should mix amiably rather than match perfectly.

Shabby-chic fabric on pillows brings color and texture to the upholstered, carved settee. Two marble-topped cast-iron tables are interesting as well as practical.

A black-and-white color scheme is most appealing in the dining room, where a dark, painted wood cabinet makes a dramatic contrast against white bead board. The original paint is worn on a rustic pine dining table surrounded by dark wood chairs.

Mismatched chairs are more interesting than a matched set and lend an informal feeling to the dining room. The colors of the sage and cream ceiling are reflected in the draperies and painting over the sideboard.

WICKER

Wicker furniture and accessories add a delightful and romantic feeling to any room, and they are perfect for the casual atmosphere of a porch. White wicker with rose-covered chintz fabric and lace-covered tables, sheer white curtains, and paintings of roses on the walls all evoke the Great Gatsby era.

Research antique wicker furniture styles before buying. Antique furniture identification and price guides can show you the different types available, as well as their current market value. Always examine the weave of antique wicker very carefully. Delicate weaves can crack and become damaged very easily, and restoring dam-

aged furniture can be costly (although a piece sometimes needs only a coat of spray paint to restore it). Antique wicker furniture is often fragile and should not be overexposed to the elements. Clean it regularly with a vacuum and a soft, damp cloth.

While real wicker furniture, even that which is gently used, is decidedly charming, it isn't always practical, and it can be expensive. However, authentic-looking copies of early pieces can be found in high-end garden shops, and very affordable wicker look-alikes are available from discounters. New wicker and rattan pieces are made over cast-aluminum, weather-resistant frames for outdoor use.

In the kitchen, where everyday meals take place, white wicker chairs surround a table from the 1970s.

CHAIRS

Vintage chairs of all varieties and uses are easy to find and lend character to any room. Even when a chair is in the worst condition, it can usually be salvaged as long as its basic lines are good. Frayed fabric can be replaced, slipcovers can hide a multitude of sins and give the shabbiest chair a lift, and wooden chairs are easy to paint.

Kitchen and Dining Chairs

Kitchen chairs seem to be ubiquitous at yard sales. Even when they are mismatched, they make a room interesting. A fresh coat of paint infuses them with

The farm table, Windsor chairs, dry sink, and plate rack—all reproductions—were the catalyst for this home's transformation. Colonial red paint works the rest of the magic.

A mid-1800s portrait of a woman hangs above a daybed found at a Paris flea market. The toile-upholstered armchair is a contemporary reproduction that marries beautifully with authentic antiques. Fabrics of different prints work well together when the colors are similar in palette.

Spindle-back dining chairs found at an estate
sale are cushioned with slipcovered pillows.
The green pine table is typical of those found
in early farmhouse kitchens.

If the cane is not in perfect condition, but a chair has a good frame, the caning can be replaced.

Caned Chairs

Cane chairs were quite popular in early homes, but they are hard to find in mint condition and it can be costly to have them repaired. You can, however, salvage the lovely original lines of a well-designed chair by refitting the seats with cushions and painting the frames to look new. Such chairs are usually delicate and graceful, and create an interesting contrast of elegant and simple when surrounding an early farmhouse table. If you find chairs in need of recaning, check in your area to see if there is a craftsperson who does this sort of work or consider doing it yourself. There are many do-it-yourself books on the market; caning kits and supplies are available through mail order houses as well as Web sites such as www.chair-caner.com.

Wing Chairs

The wing chair was a staple in early American homes. Introduced to America in the eighteenth century, the wing chair,

new life and a youthful energy—mixing colors adds interest and a bit of fun to your kitchen's décor. If you find a set of matching dining chairs in perfect condition, you might pair them with a painted farmhouse table for an informal look. Pine kitchen tables were staples in Early American homes across the country. Whether you find a set or just one, a kitchen or dining chair can be painted and softened with a cushion covered in new or vintage fabric. A typical country look is simple to achieve by adding a blue and white checked cushion to a white painted chair.

CANE WORK

In Europe, the popularity of cane as a seating material has remained constant since the seventeenth century. Even today a good percentage of modern furniture includes some cane work, either for its decorative qualities or for its practicality. If you have patience, cane work can be a fascinating and productive hobby, and there are many books and catalogs for supplies available.

An old wing chair is transformed with vintage fabrics, trims of old lace, and looped ribbon.

originally called a grandfather chair (and later an easy chair) endures as a favorite piece of furniture. Both in America and England, a wing chair covered in fabric was a comfortable necessity as well as a status symbol. Keeping warm in Colonial America required creativity; homes were drafty, even with oilcloth hung on walls for insulation. What began in the 1600s as a type of chair for the elderly and infirm evolved in the New World as a refuge for every household member—the perfect place to keep warm. Cushioned, fabric-covered wings that sheltered the occupant blocked drafts while retaining the warmth generated by

fires, and people often took meals in a wing chair pulled up to the fireplace.

Because craftsmen of the day used regional wood to fashion the frames, the woods used often indicate a chair's place of origin. For example, local cypress was used in Charleston, South Carolina, while in places like Boston, Philadelphia, New York, and Newport, Rhode Island,

The windows are the only giveaway that the house is new. All the furnishings are either authentic antiques or very good contemporary reproductions. Carefully selected fabrics are key to creating the right mix.

The overall form of a frame tells you much about its date and period, and often where it was made; look at the sweep of the wings and for carved details such as ball-and-claw feet. The finished fabric follows the form of the chair and makes it beautiful.

Once you've learned a bit about the different styles of wing chairs it is not necessary to search for an antique if it is out of your price range. Reproductions are readily available and found in most furniture stores today. You will be able to find one in a style suited to your taste and the style of your room.

Windsor Chairs

The American version of a Windsor chair originated as garden chairs in Rhode Island circa 1790. With their characteristic slender spindles and curved saddle seats, they soon became de rigueur in the kitchens and dining rooms of early America. Windsor chairs were crafted from a mix of woods, then painted rather than stained. There are many different styles as well as prices. Reproductions are available from such furniture stores as Ethan Allen for around three hundred dollars, but you can also find a simple budget version of the most popular Windsor side chair, the bow-back, at Target, for less than seventy dollars.

the chair frames were made from white pine, maple, and birch. Mahogany was expensive and used sparingly, for conspicuous elements.

When looking for a wing chair, do not be put off if the fabric is worn or frayed; it is easy and relatively inexpensive (depending on the fabric you choose) to re-cover such a chair, and an inferior wing chair can look good dressed in a luxurious fabric. When wing chairs first appeared in American homes, fabric was the chief expense in their manufacture. Today, however, the value of an original Chippendale, Queen Anne, Federal, or Georgian wing chair is all in its bones.

Kitchen chairs are easy to find at yard sales. A new coat of paint is all that's needed. Farmhouse chairs, spray painted in pastel colors have a vintage flair.

The eighteenth-century pine dining table is pegged. The top can flip up to become a high-backed bench. The reproduction cabinet holds a collection of early pewter, and the Windsor chairs compliment a blue cabinet. Here the new pieces mix well with the old.

BEDS

The bed is usually the focal point of a bedroom; it might therefore be the one antique item in the room. Or you might opt for a reproduction of an early bed and use vintage linens and quilts on top. You don't need an Early American bed frame to create a vintage look, but many homeowners like the idea of sleeping in a bed that originally resided in a bedroom in the eighteen hundreds. Antique iron beds have something you simply can't find in a newly made piece of furniture: character and a past. The one thing you can't get from an antique bed is a frame large enough for a queen- or king-size mattress; most are twins or doubles, and some are the size of a daybed. (These can, however, function as a charming substitute for a love seat in a living room or an accent in a dining or family room.) Antique lace coverlets and piles of pillows add to the romantic feeling of these beds for a decidedly vintage approach to decorating the bedroom.

Four-poster beds offer another option, both as an antique or a reproduction. Headboards once tended to be plain because the drapery that kept out drafts covered them up. New headboards tend to be more decorative, although still less so than posts. Some manufacturers of new beds employ antique parts (antique posts **might** be used with newly crafted frames, for example) to make them look old.

SALVAGE SAVVY

Give your home character with an infusion of salvaged material reused as artistic elements. You'll find treasures rescued from condemned buildings throughout the country that span America's architectural heritage from 1730 to the 1950s. Louvered doors, fireplace mantels, hinges, doorknobs and other hardware, barn doors, a handrail from an old bar, stained-glass windows, radiators ready for a second

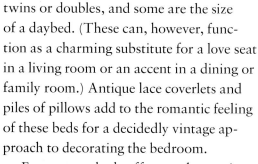

A nineteenth-century rope bed in a guest bedroom is painted with a red stain. The crazy quilt is an antique from the Victorian era , but the hooked rug is a reproduction copied from a primitive design.

A trundle rope bed is the centerpiece of the bedroom. Its wooden wheels are thought to be derivative of Shaker style. Braided rugs like this new one were often found in early homes, as were quilts—such as this patchwork cover—which were usually made from worn clothing. Chandeliers throughout the house are reproductions of the period.

FOUR-POSTER BEDS

A four-poster bed is one with four vertical columns, one in each corner, that support a tester, or upper (usually rectangular) panel. There are a number of antique four-poster beds dating to the sixteenth century and earlier, many of which are highly ornate and made from oak.

The function of the tester was usually to hold bed curtains that could surround the bed to keep out drafts. In the modern Western world, this function became unnecessary because of improvements in insulation. Consequently, the posts and tester became a redundant element of comfortable bedding, and their cost made them gradually less and less popular. Nevertheless, the four-poster bed without the tester has remained a popular style for many bedrooms because of its traditional, luxurious look.

There are many styles of four-poster beds. If you can't find or afford an original, it's easy to substitute a reproduction for the same look.

life, a 1920s wrought-iron door, Dutch doors, staircase spindles, hefty brass strap hinges, even a church steeple—these are just some of the oddities homeowners have reclaimed as decorative objects to reuse in creative ways. You may not know exactly how you're going to use something at the time you discover it, but if it appeals to you, it's worth purchasing and saving it until the inspiration hits. (It's better than later saying, "If only I had scooped up that piece of molding when I had the chance.") Always be on the lookout for interesting pieces and then look for inventive ways to use what you find.

A canopy bed gives dramatic stature to the once-cramped and uninteresting master bedroom. Natural cotton bed hangings with a damask scroll weave and a colorful crewelwork coverlet replicate what finer homes in the 1750s might have had.

ARCHITECTURAL AND VINTAGE DETAILS

A claw-foot bathtub is a stylish center-piece in any bathroom. Whether you are designing your bathroom with a classic vintage theme or you simply want to add a vintage flair to a contemporary design, claw-foot tubs are both luxurious and practical. Designs such as slipper and double-slipper tubs provide for a truly elegant bathing experience, while the nos-talgic designs of classic roll-rim and flat-rim claw-foot tubs are reminiscent of days

A "found" painting hangs over an office "desk." The lamp and chandelier are flea market finds.

A mélange of vintage objects include an un-usual hexagonal mirrored frame.

gone by. Pedestal bathtubs and double-ended claw-foot tubs are other popular styles that find their way into a variety of vintage bathroom remodeling projects.

And remember, things don't always have to be used as originally intended. For example, one homeowner likes to hang architectural pieces such as bits of

In the bedroom, the patina, shapes, and proportions of the lamp, alarm clock, and phone create a pleasing arrangement on top of a rare Florentine chest. An oversize painting completes the scene.

Layered linens make the bed as graceful as a Victorian dress, starting with an "underslip" of matelassé and moving up to a chenille blanket and white lace throw, perhaps once a tablecloth.

elaborate plaster molding on the wall as art. Another found an early wooden tub at a flea market: It became the perfect base for a coffee table. Industrial design elements, weathered signs, and metal fixtures add personality and style to a country kitchen, as do doorknobs when used as cabinet knobs. Metal objects age in amazing ways. The longer you keep them, the better they look.

If it's worn, white, crackled, and peeling, it has old-world charm. Nothing should be perfect or pristine. If you are lucky enough to find a discarded church pew, it could serve as an unusual replacement for dining room chairs. Porch posts make interesting dining table legs. Vintage frames in different sizes and shapes can be fitted with mirrors to capture light and give a room old-world elegance. A pediment from a doorway to an old house or elements salvaged from a church might flank living room windows. If your space is limited, try layering upward by using architectural elements to punctuate walls and shelves. Garden furniture that is light and airy and a wrought-iron table with a glass top are good choices for indoor use. In the end, it isn't the structure you live in, it's what you do with it that makes it a home.

WROUGHT-IRON FURNITURE

Wrought-iron furniture was used as far back as the Roman Empire. Beds were a favorite in Victorian times; wrought-iron garden furniture was first used in the eighteenth century. Decorative wrought iron features fancy designs such as fleurs-de-lis and elaborate floral designs, while cast-iron furniture has very little decoration, except for features like the turnings on bed posts. Early wrought-iron garden furniture will usually have some rusted parts. These can be left as is or spray painted with a rust-retardant enamel.

In a small space, wrought-iron garden furniture, with its glass top and airy lines, looks lighter than solid furniture.

Weathered football benches, stacked to create shelves, hold books and favorite objects. Ivory denim cushions that unzip for the wash make elegant antique chairs practical. Suitcases can be used for storage as well as an end table.

Vintage mirrors line a stairwell, adding sparkle and interest to the wall.

Anything blue will do. The shelves include spongeware and transferware alongside bottles with blue labels, soap boxes, and mixing bowls.

PUTTING IT TOGETHER

What makes decorating in an early style work is how you put the furnishings, accessories, and colors together. The most successful projects give old style a fresh look that doesn't seem stuck in another era.

Many older homes often seem dark because of the paint colors and dark wood furnishings. It is refreshing to find dark wood or painted furniture

The rose painting is displayed on a reproduction white dresser.

Printed fabrics in a soft pink cover the pillows on the antique white iron bed, creating a shabby-chic effect. A butterfly pin adds interest to one of the pillows.

pieces in light-colored rooms. It can be most appealing when the furnishings are arranged in a neutral setting. The emphasis in your house might be on textures and shapes that show up best against light-colored walls. Consider finding an Early American cupboard to fill with vintage linens in various shades of cream. Pair wood furniture with the softness of upholstered pieces in cream-colored homespun and vintage linens to make your rooms seem contemporary with vintage overtones—a decidedly understated style. The neutral palette will make your house feel at once up-to-date and homey. Touches of fresh green found in organic accessories such as plants in wooden buckets or Granny Smith apples piled in a wooden bowl on the coffee table infuse rooms with just the right amount of color. To go with this look throughout

Claw-foot tubs are among the most coveted salvaged objects for creating a vintage-looking bathroom. The Kohler Company makes reproductions if you can't find or afford an original.

the house, keep your floors bare, save for perhaps a woven area rug in the living room or an occasional small hooked rug in another room. Crisp white napkins bring elegance to a worn, painted, even crude table, for an interesting contraposition.

Now that you've seen how to mix antiques with reproduction furniture, consider a more contemporary approach—combine them with a few modern things. A nineteenth-century black painted cupboard might be filled with white chinaware and crystal glasses for a dramatic black-and-white color scheme in the dining room. Consider filling a white ceramic pitcher with fresh cut flowers that look as though they came from a cottage garden. This small, inexpensive accessory will provide color, freshness, and a lived-in feeling, and the color you introduce to a black-and-white scheme in this way can be easily changed with the seasons. Embrace such contrasts.

A lace-covered table is surrounded with elegant reproduction distressed chairs upholstered in white damask. White dinnerware, candlesticks, mirror frames, a sideboard, and two crystal chandeliers create a dreamy dining room. Pink candles and a white pitcher of roses punctuate this soft palette with pale color.

4

COLLECTIONS

A collection is a group of similar things, usually artfully arranged. There are no specific criteria for collecting something, and a collection doesn't have to be worth a lot of money: creative people know how to make an interesting display of their collectibles.

Collecting things from the past is an easy, often affordable way to give a new house old-house charm. A collection with a historic connection is more interesting and meaningful, and collectibles that are antiques are not necessarily expensive; look for the things

A wall of shelves holds an impressive collection of pastel Lu-Ray pottery, with vintage pillows below.

that appeal to you, fit in with your décor, and are within your budget. Remember, a collection can be acquired over time.

ACCIDENTAL COLLECTIONS

Many collections start by accident. Perhaps you bought a Toby mug at a flea market, then another at a yard sale, and now you find yourself looking for Toby mugs wherever you travel. Or maybe someone gave you an early piece of pottery or a lovely creamware bowl, sparking your interest in similar items. A collection can start with anything that attracts your interest, for whatever reason.

COLLECTING
PIECE BY PIECE

Bead board is used inside the kitchen cupboards, and the shelves display a collection of mismatched chinaware—some current, some from the past.

A collection is usually not purchased as a whole, but rather collected piece by piece. That's the fun of collecting: first you have the experience of finding a new piece, and then the experience of seeing it displayed with the rest of the collection. There's no end to the number of pieces you can add, and each piece is a reminder of a different time and place, when and where the item was purchased.

Black books and Asian-style pedestals foster a study in contrasts. The white cabinet provides the perfect setting for this collection.

The bedroom is a mélange of pastel colors, from the stenciled wall to the yo-yo coverlet on the bed.

A well-loved teddy
bear snuggles with
a tiny companion on
a late eighteenth-
century youth chair.

PERSONALIZED COLLECTIONS

A collection is an individual statement. The things in a collection are highly personal and give homes personality and character. They have a story to tell, but often what's most interesting is the story the collections tell about their owners—the story of how these things made their way into the hands of their collectors and the feelings they inspire.

Some of the items people collect include mid- to late-nineteenth-century maps, coral and shells (beachcombed and bought both old and new), walking sticks and canes, alarm clocks, and apothecary jars (many filled with shells, buttons, or spools of thread). Some people like to specialize their collections—for example, a collection of kitchen-related items that includes canisters, canning jars, coffee grinders, and antique scales.

Many people are attracted to Early American objects, which lend an air of stability to a new home. The following are some ideas about Early American collectibles and ephemera and how to display them in your new home.

1. Oversize crocks to fill a niche of shelves.
2. Antique mechanical toys displayed on narrow shelves.
3. Old black-and-white photographs of family members, all framed with narrow black frames, lining a narrow wall area.
4. Teddy bears arranged playfully around a room as if they were perfectly at home. One might sit in a child's high chair, another propped in a bookshelf, and still another tucked into the arm of a sofa.
5. Small wooden boxes of all sorts with interesting fittings and handles— some grouped, others stacked, larger ones on the floor. All should be used to hold something, so they are useful as well as decorative.

A Mason jar is filled with a collection of strawberry pincusions from the late 1800s and tomato pincushions from the 1940s.

6. Baskets hanging from a rafter or beam, or lined up on a bench or shelf, always within easy access so they can be put to practical use.

7. Glass oil lamps or pretty vases grouped on top of a highboy or sideboard in a dining room, near enough to a window to catch the light.

8. Quilts on beds, as wall hangings or table covers, and over a sofa or chair. The good parts of damaged quilts can be used to cover pillows.

9. Early samplers framed simply and grouped on one wall or over a fireplace.

10. Early American tools mounted and carefully arranged on a wall.

11. Carefully arranged books with old leather bindings filling an entire wall as the focal point of an otherwise stark and uncluttered room. (Great for the soul!)

12. A collection of shells in a rustic Indian basket on a table—simple and lovely. The shells' different natural colors, shapes, and patterns come together to create a work of art as nice as any you could buy.

DISPLAYING COLLECTIONS

It's one thing to be obsessed with collecting; it's another knowing how to arrange a collection so that it is shown to its best advantage. Many collectors have developed a passion for how to display what they collect, making their homes the ultimate gallery. Items that were once purely functional often become art. The following are one seasoned collector's top tips and rules for collecting and displaying.

An interest in collecting things from the past sparked a desire to create a retro kitchen in which to showcase them.

• *Money Isn't Everything:* Buy for looks, not necessarily for value. If something turns out to appreciate in value, great—but in the long run, aesthetics matter more.

• *Shop Strategically:* Big shows tend to bring big prices. Find a local market (limit yourself to a one-hour drive) big enough to attract a mix of vendors but still offer deals.

• *Buy by the Lot:* You can often work out a better deal by buying an entire lot—just make sure the value of the items justifies the cost.

• *Build Relationships:* Try to buy in local markets where you know the sellers and they know what you like.

• *Educate Yourself:* Go to as many antiques shows and flea markets as you can. The Web is a great tool for finding information on a particular item quickly and for checking prices.

• *Have Fun with Displays:* Vary height and depth. Don't just line up items; put different sizes together, create elevations, stack objects on top of each other, or arrange them sideways.

• *Embrace the Eco-Friendly:* There is no better recycling than antiques—when something that would have ended up in a landfill becomes art.

• *Maintain Accessibility:* Keep displays contained, controlled, and accessible for cleaning.

A melange of vintage collectibles create a personal display.

White matte finishes link a ceramics collection composed of a variety of styles, ages, and designs. Floor-to-ceiling shelving keeps it all organized.

MIX AND MATCH COLLECTIONS

Collections are as varied as the people who collect them, and there is no rhyme or reason to why one person collects pottery and another pincushions. Some people have a knack for displaying their collections and know how to incorporate them into their everyday lives. Others simply arrange them as decorative objects.

A couple from Portland, Oregon, share a passion for all things vintage but live in a sleek new town house. Their collections of ceramics, furniture, and spirited accessories are showcased beautifully against its clean lines and white walls, making everything sculptural. Their 1,500-square-foot space manages to look up-to-date and orderly due to artful arranging and floor-to-ceiling shelves. Rather than concentrating on pricey, pedigreed items, they pride themselves on finding inexpensive and interesting things before they become the rage.

Another homeowner with a similar passion for collecting all-white pottery says, "Collections make a room." His collections of Southern pottery, Native American baskets, and other country antiques are positioned in each room of

It takes a trained eye to combine different textures, both elegant and rustic, in all shades of white. A jumble of lace-covered pillows on a linen hammock, a crystal chandelier, and a zebra rug are unexpectedly paired on a screened-in porch. The whitewashed pine table is another unusual find.

WHITE IRONSTONE

The simple lines of ironstone are quite appealing, and its neutral palette goes with all decorating styles. White ironstone china was first made in Staffordshire, England, in 1813. It was harder than earthenware and stronger than porcelain. Some of these wares were decorated with transfer patterns or brush strokes. In 1842 the first white ironstone china was marketed to Americans, who preferred the plain, unfussy version. Late in the 1850s and into the 1860s, ironstone was decorated with wheat, prairie flowers, and corn to appeal to farmers, who fed the large numbers of farmhands helping with their harvests; it was sold in large quantities in agricultural communities across the country.

Worn metal or wood is paired with soft furnishings. The canopy is from an old store display, and hanging below it are the pearls, beads, hats, and bags of the homeowner's grandmother.

his house. Far from being merely finishing touches, the cherished objects are an integral part of the décor. The biggest and most impressive collection is a dazzling array of white ironstone pitchers, teapots, coffeepots, compotes, and platters, all housed in an 1870s cupboard. The red interior of the cupboard provides a perfect backdrop to show them off dramatically.

Tricks for Storing and Displaying

1. Keep like things together for a strong visual impact.
2. A large grouping is more interesting than a small one. Make it look significant.
3. Floor-to-ceiling shelving is a good way to show off a collection. Painting shelves white highlights the objects they display.
4. Identify one standout feature to make a pleasing rather than distracting display: arrange a collection by one strong color, for example, or display objects all made of the same material.

A stack of home-made storage boxes, painted with blue and green buttermilk paints, sits above an apothecary chest, next to a collection of rustic game boards.

Painted Talavera pottery, Bauer pottery, and Fiestaware are enjoyed through everyday use.

endeavor, it's a challenge to find the right elements. So she transfers dry goods to plain glass jars, buys shampoo based on the bottle's hue, uses white toothbrushes, and plants white flowers. She says this heightens her discrimination for the pieces she chooses to own. Textures and shapes, such as those found in baskets, introduce warmth without detracting from the color scheme. Industrial wire is appreciated for its simple form, and shells and horn for their luster. Then she groups things in odd numbers and off center.

The collection began with the discovery of one white ironstone pitcher, found in an antiques store. In a relatively short period of time, the collector amassed hundreds of additional examples.

Creating a quiet style, another homeowner in Minnesota chose a palette of only white, brown, black, and silver. While the limited spectrum of colors certainly makes coordinating an easier

A stack of old suitcases are tagged to let the owner know what is stored inside each one.

Green Floraline ceramics from the 1950s come in a variety of different sizes and shapes, adding to the interest of this collection.

Although the kitchen was completely renovated, the painted Texas hanging cupboard (circa 1900) was used among the new cabinetry and appliances and houses the ironstone collection.

A LOVE OF QUILTS

Nothing is quite so evocative of Early American homes as a patchwork or appliqué quilt. Quilts make wonderful displays because they are textural, colorful, and useful. Childhood memories provide a continual source of inspiration for many collectors who fill their homes with early quilts amassed since they were quite young. "We always had quilts on our beds growing up," says one collector, "so displaying them in my own home brings me close to my family." Her favorite colors are associated with the flowers grown in her mother's garden; a particular favorite is pink, to match the peonies that filled the garden each summer.

Practical as well as pretty, quilts offer emotional comfort. A collection of quilts can be both admired and enjoyed for warmth on chilly evenings—and can be used for all sorts of creative decorating. Try hanging a quilt over the balustrade of a stairwell. Layers of quilts can also be used on beds, and more quilts can be displayed on a traditional quilt rack. Collectors use quilts on beds and as table covers, and hang them on walls. Because crib quilts are small, they can be hung as textile paintings in spaces that cannot accommodate full-size quilts.

Quilts have been one of the more collected objects of folk art in this country because Early American quilt patterns are surprisingly timeless in design. Ever appealing, the original, naively conceived quilt patterns are still being reproduced by manufacturers,

Collectors have their favorite patterns and color combinations. Blue and white quilts are particularly sought after and look pretty folded and stacked on a rustic bench in an entryway.

A quilt is the perfect foil for disguising a worn sofa with style and cozy comfort. Topped with a jumble of pillows, it practically begs for someone to curl up with a good book.

and copied and reinterpreted by modern quiltmakers over and over again to this day. These designs were graphic in nature and therefore offer endless opportunity for improvisation in color, pattern, and size. Almost all the shapes are geometric and therefore didn't require an artist to render. Because early quilters weren't designers, but rather simple housewives,

CARING FOR QUILTS

Whether you have an old or new quilt, it deserves care and preservation. Light exposure, moisture, mildew, moths, and improper storage will harm any quilt. While quilts made by Early American women were originally intended to be used and washed often, many dealers feel that frequent washing deteriorates the fabric. They suggest shaking the dust from quilts instead, and occasionally vacuuming them with light suction.

Never store quilts in plastic bags. It's best to roll them around acid-free tubes and wrap them in acid-free tissue paper. They need to breathe. Alternatives to tissue paper are cotton sheets or lengths of prewashed muslin. If a quilt is stored away for any length of time, it's best to shake it out occasionally and refold it in another direction to avoid creating sharp creases. Of course, the best way to keep a quilt looking good is not to store it away at all: simply spread it on a seldom-used bed and shake it out now and then.

they found inspiration in what they saw from their windows—bear footprints in the snow, a log cabin, flying geese, a rose of Sharon, flowers, log cabin fence rails—and brought that inspiration to life with cut pieces of fabric.

New quilts are just as lovely as—and less expensive than—antique quilts. Over time and with several washings, they will acquire a soft and faded look, as if they were antiques.

VINTAGE FABRICS

Vintage fabrics bring a lived-in element to any room and should mix amiably rather than match perfectly. When used on pillows they bring color and texture to a white room. Don't overlook or discard a worn quilt that appears to be beyond repair. It can be cut up to make into pillow covers, with a new piece of fabric for the backing. Remnants of fabrics that look old can be found in fabric shops.

Here are some ideas for adding comfortable elegance to any sofa:

1. For an extravagant look, cover pillows with remnants of upholstery fabric.
2. Use calico fabrics for instant country charm.
3. Homespun fabric is reminiscent of Early American households.
4. Soft, worn, printed cotton sheeting creates a shabby-chic look.
5. An old chenille bedspread is perfect for turning into vintage pillow covers.
6. Combine prints, stripes, and checks for an interesting look. Try to find fabrics with faded colors of the same value.

To give new fabric a soft, worn look, wash it with a small amount of bleach and then rinse with fabric softener. For instant aging, rinse fabric in a tea bath.

The stair railing is the perfect place to display several colorful quilts of similar patterns. Two quilts hang on the white painted walls, while a lineup of English blue glass bottles sparkle on the sills, reflecting sunlight.

VINTAGE LINENS

In eighteenth-century England, a tea towel was a special linen drying cloth used by the mistress of the house to dry her precious—and expensive—china tea things. Retro fabrics with prints such as cherries and bouquets of flowers have been reproduced, and it is easy to make your own vintage kitchen accessories.

New windows allow light to flood the dining room, and the worn painted apothecary cabinet, put to practical use holding linens, adds old-world character. Freshly picked white hydrangeas fill an old wooden barrel.

CHENILLE BEDSPREADS

The technique of tufting emerged in the 1890s in Dalton, Georgia, and played an important role in the economic development of the northwestern part of the state. The process involved cotton sheeting, to which handcrafters applied designs with raised tufts of thick yarn. The tufted bedspreads they made were often referred to as chenille, the French word for "caterpillar," which is generally used to describe fabrics that have a thick pile protruding all around at right angles. By the 1920s tufted bedspreads appeared on shelves of department stores in Atlanta, New York, Philadelphia, and other major cities. The production of these products was responsible for feeding many rural farm families during the Great Depression.

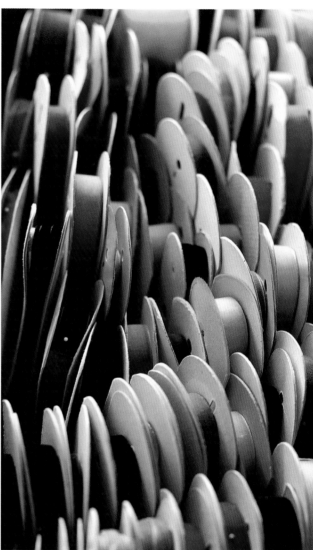

A collection of 129 handcrafted velvet ribbon spools.

It doesn't matter what the pattern or colors are, vintage fabrics will always look good in a room.

PERIOD PASTELS

Pastel chinaware is a vintage accessory that looks good on display and is extremely practical as well. Fiestaware and Lu-Ray and McCoy pottery were all at the peak of their popularity in the 1950s. Today these pieces often show up at flea markets. If this pottery appeals to you, consider painting the walls of your home in shades of lavender, sea foam green, or yellow.

The Taylor, Smith & Taylor Company manufactured Lu-Ray pottery from 1938 to 1961. The four original colors were surf green, Windsor blue, Sharon pink, and Persian cream, which was actually soft yellow. A fifth color, Chatham gray, was introduced in 1949. It was

Lu-Ray plates made before the early 1950s are stamped with the manufacturer's initials and the date each was made.

never as popular as the others and was discontinued around 1952. All pieces produced before the early 1950s are stamped on the back, "TS&T Lu-Ray Pastels USA," followed by numbers representing the month and year in which the piece was made. This pottery is similar to Fiestaware and McCoy pottery made around the same period and popular for everyday use. (See page 82 for more about Fiestaware).

For a display, fill shelves and cupboards with a variety of pastel pottery, trays, framed floral paintings, and containers filled with buttons and spools of silk thread. A grouping of pottery hanging on

Part of a collection of pastel Shawnee miniatures.

The dining room is filled with vintage collections, including a cupboard of all-white pottery and a wall of floral paintings.

walls is another nice way to display these objects. One homeowner who collects and decorates with pottery (her collection tops six hundred pieces!) says pink is the hardest color to find. One wall in her breakfast nook displays the array of pottery with like pieces in varying colors grouped on each shelf. A sofa below is filled with pillows that echo the colors but introduce patterns for interest.

It's a good idea to mix some soft items with the pottery in a room. For example, one homeowner likes to display early quilts (such as a colorful yo-yo coverlet) in her bedroom, with pillows in the various pastel colors found in the quilt patterns. A crocheted granny square afghan covers a bench, and a prized oil painting from a garage sale rests on a ledge on the harlequin-painted wall.

A collection of Wild Rose and Blossom Time McCoy pottery fills corner shelves in the living room.

PLATES

A collection of plates on a wall is a simple way to introduce texture, patterns, and a chosen color scheme for very little expense. Plates of similar style, color, or period make an interesting focal point in an early cupboard or on open shelves. Plates are like art. They add a focal point to any room, and grouped together or integrated with other objects such as a mirror, they draw interest.

Many people think an all-white palette of plates is uninteresting, but in reality it is easy to live with. When you create a collection of accessories limited to white, the choices are quick and easy to make. By introducing soft, light-toned woods, you will create warmth and relieve the room of starkness. Some collectors choose a black-and-white palette that gives a plate collection a modern point of view, even though they are vintage.

A white upholstered sofa is the beginning of a black-and-white palette in the living room. A wall of black-framed artwork and a black-and-white signs make a bold statement and further accentuate the color scheme.

Hanging a Plate Collection

Hanging plates does not require any special skill. Most people choose plates to hang according to design or theme, or to match the color scheme of a room. Plates can be hung in rows, in a square or rectangle, or in a circle, with four plates creating the rim and one plate in the center. The plates in a grouping don't need to

A grouping of artwork framed in black is artfully arranged to create a collection.

CHINTZWARE

Chintzware became a popular china pattern in the early part of the twentieth century, when artisans would cut a pattern from floral lithographs and apply it to a dish or cup. The china with an all-over flower pattern has since been produced around the world. The most sought-after pieces are from Staffordshire, England. Today's collectors each have their favorite patterns—and there are literally hundreds to choose from.

---

match (in fact, it's often more interesting if they don't). You can even mix antique and modern plates; it's best, however, to make an arrangement with plates of the same size and shape.

Create an arrangement over a small table in an entryway, or use plates to balance the weight of the furnishings by grouping them next to a chair or chest. Unlike paintings, plates provide dimensionality; they can also add pattern and sometimes even surprise to the walls of a room.

A stack of firkins fills a corner of the dining room. The chandelier is a reproduction as are the chairs surrounding the pine table.

A display of blue and white floral plates and cobalt glasses and mugs adds to a bold color scheme in the kitchen. Vintage wicker lends a warm, natural touch.

The texture and spottiness of quail eggs is especially lovely as a display in a white bowl and is in keeping with the homeowner's philosophy: a house shouldn't be about perfection.

CREAMWARE

Creamware is a type of pottery that originated in England in the late eighteenth century. It was designed as a substitute for Chinese porcelain and launched the career of Josiah Wedgwood. In the mid-1760s, Wedgwood developed a very refined form of earthenware, with a cream-colored glaze whose shade varied from piece to piece; he called it queensware. The cream-

Small silver salt shakers, white ironstone platters, and a mix of creamware is part of a collection housed in a painted white cabinet. It is used often—a sign of a good collection—and serves a purpose beyond visual enjoyment.

ware made by the Leeds Pottery Company had a greenish tint.

Creamware was first made in raised patterns of basket weave or pierced leaf. Wedgwood pieces are prized for their fine shapes and creamy glaze. Many creamware pieces were printed with transfer designs, but plain creamware made between 1767 and 1790, with designs in shallow relief or with punched designs, remains the most in demand. The forms are endless—from candlesticks and elaborate cruet sets to simple plates.

A collection of creamware found a fitting home in this faded blue antique hutch lined with toile.

BUTTONS

Bone was one of the earliest materials used to make buttons—they have been found in Egyptian tombs dating back to the Sixth Dynasty. In the seventeenth century it was common for European porcelain manufacturers to make buttons. Josiah Wedgwood made cameo-like buttons. Crocheted buttons were popular in France and Ireland. Fine glass buttons were introduced in the eighteenth century, and Britain's Queen Victoria popularized black glass buttons worn on mourning clothes.

Leather buttons were made by bookbinders and shoemakers. Plastic buttons became popular in 1872 with the invention of celluloid. Today, the most popular buttons with collectors are made of Bakelite, which was invented between 1907 and 1909. Whimsical buttons were made around 1938, and in America, satin buttons were popular for ladies' garments.

HOOKED ON RUGS

Rug hooking has a history that spans over 150 years in this country and is considered to be one of America's few indigenous crafts, having originated in northeast New England and the Maritime Provinces of Canada.

Many of the earliest hooked rugs that survive today came from maritime settlements. The long, inactive periods at sea led to the invention of a primitive form of rug hooking in which sailors used bits of raveled burlap to create marine scenes on a rough linen background. In all probability, true rug hooking as the craft is now defined evolved when a sailor's wife, admiring her husband's handiwork, decided to use old materials around the house in a similar fashion. Her subject matter—hearth and home—reflected her surroundings rather than those of her seafaring mate.

The earliest rug hookers were uninhibited when it came to drawing their subjects. This is evidenced in a lack of concern for accuracy of scale and perspective. Animals are often distorted and flowers frequently drawn larger than the houses in the same scene. This is the very quality that makes these early rugs

A collection of antique photographs and button accents adorn this wall.

Family pets inspired many a hooked-rug project. This nineteenth-century rug is affixed to a frame for display on a wall and appreciated for its uninhibited interpretation. It is a charming example of American folk art.

such desirable and interesting pieces of folk art. New England hooked rugs were often made with the same calico fabrics found in early quilts, and the garden was a great source of design inspiration. From the 1850s to the 1870s, folk artists executed their own floral, geometric, and pictorial designs. Some of the most popular images were of farm animals and birds, the American eagle being a perennial favorite.

From the 1850s until the 1930s, rug hooking became somewhat of a craze among American housewives. They carried on and perfected the technique, which flourished as a practical as well as recreational pastime. Families and friends often got together for "rug frolics"—the equivalent of quilting bees. Just as our early homemakers pieced together scraps of fabric from worn-out clothing to make patchwork quilts, strips of worn clothing, such as a woolen coat, were used to create hooked rugs.

Caring for Hooked Rugs

To determine the condition of an old rug, hold it up to the light. If it's filled with holes, it may have dry rot and will surely fall apart. This sort of disrepair is impossible to fix. An old rug that is too delicate to use can be bound and mounted for framing. If you have a rug that needs restoring, find someone who knows what they're doing, preferably a fine sewer.

Don't vacuum the rug, but rather place it face down and sweep it. Periodically sun and air rugs. And never shake an old rug: The burlap on which early rugs were first hooked (modern hookers use a sturdy canvas) is much weaker than the wool and often disintegrates.

Wash a rug a section at a time using a soft brush and cold, slightly soapy water. Do not wring it out or hang it up to dry. With the front side facing out, roll the rug in a heavy towel to absorb the moisture, and then roll it out flat to dry. To store a rug, roll it with the front side out and wrap it with a sheet or cloth for protection.

A rug that is used on the floor will last longer and stay in better condition if you put it on top of another carpet or use a rubber pad beneath it. Keep valuable and delicate rugs out of high-traffic areas. Dirt, mud, spills, and sunlight are enemies of your hooked rugs.

Like quilts, hooked rugs have a humble origin. Early hooked rugs are appreciated for their simple, artistic appeal and because they speak of a gentler, less complex time in history. The hooked rug is a visual testament of the way life used to be. These charming examples of naive creative expression tell much about life in the nineteenth and early twentieth centuries. It is only in recent times, however, that the hooked rug has been appreciated as an important part of America's heritage. As with quilts, hooked rugs began life as strictly utilitarian, and people tended to take them for granted, never thinking to elevate them to the status of an art form. With the growing interest in American folk art has come an appreciation for their design, craftsmanship, and historic value. Collecting early hooked rugs links the present to the past and adds a dimension of Early American character to a home.

A pair of plush ducks occupies a 24-inch square rug that dates from the 1920s. Early hooked rugs are appreciated for their naive lack of accuracy and drawing perspective.

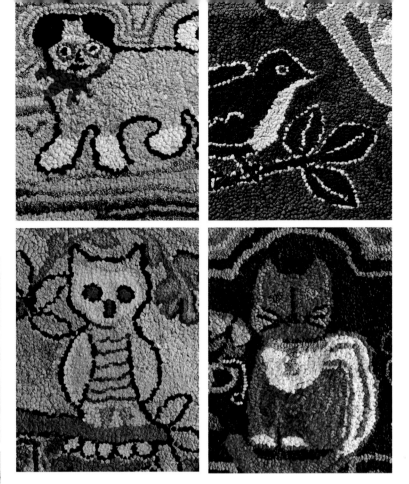

Left: The disproportional size of the bird to the branch is part of this circa 1900 folk rug's appeal, and one of the reasons for its value.

Above: Subjects of creatures often found in early rugs include: a diminutive owl (1920s), a perching blackbird (1930s), a perky pooch (1940s), and a whimsical red cat (circa 1900s). Family pets were often the subjects for illustrations on early hooked rugs.

This 1950s-era pointer poised against a New England landscape was hooked onto a pre-stamped foundation, a process developed in 1868 by a Maine peddler named Edward Sands Frost.

RETRO COLLECTIONS

For some collectors, specific kinds of objects hold appeal, and they concentrate on finding as many of them as possible. Other collectors zero in on a particular period, such as the 1940s or 1950s, and are dedicated to decorating their entire house in collectibles and furnishings of that era.

It might start with a piece of vintage fabric, which leads to another; before long, you have a huge collection. These yardages, and even curtain panels, are tailor-made for filling rooms with color and patterns reminiscent of the forties and fifties.

Some collectors like to immerse themselves in the style that reminds them of their grandparents' house. One such collector has this advice to impart: "Collect what you love and figure out a way to make it work." By relying on particular objects, colors, and textures, you can achieve a vintage look. Don't know where to start? Begin with a color scheme. For example, the forties and fifties were known for a candy-pink and mint-green palette. You might find a green painted piece of furniture, such as a bureau, that dictates the paint color for the guest bedroom walls. Colorful vintage tablecloths take on a new role as window toppers, and a chenille bedspread might be converted to a shower curtain. Funky printed textiles, classic rattan, mid-century American pottery, even a myriad of kitsch can all be thrown into the retro mix.

Turquoise was a popular hue in the 1950s. When designing a kitchen, you might take cues from old fifties wares such as Pyrex bowls and printed tablecloths that lead to the introduction of another color: red. A painted wooden cupboard might hold a plethora of turquoise pottery that includes McCoy pieces. When you go antiquing, fine-tune your vision so that anything from the fifties pops out at you.

Little things like the green glass, pottery, and canisters imbue a room with **personality.**

A guest bedroom faithfully adheres to the candy-pink and mint-green colors so popular in the 1950s.

KITSCH

Of German origin, the word kitsch, which came into use in the nineteenth century, has been used to categorize art that is considered to be a tasteless copy of an existing style. It was originally associated with art that is sentimental. Today, garden gnomes and other lawn ornaments are often considered kitschy, as is a collection of Cupie dolls. Such items, while looked down upon by serious art collectors, are highly desirable among retro collectors.

Turquoise was a popular color in the 1950s. In the kitchen, a homeowner arranged a collection of turquoise-colored pottery on a cupboard shelf. Some of the pieces are McCoy.

When redesigning her kitchen, this home owner took cues from old 1950s ware such as Pyrex bowls and printed tablecloths. The metal dinette set is typical of the era.

EVERYDAY ITEMS

Need a great way to display collectibles and add character to a room? Start with one great piece of furniture, such as a cupboard or sideboard. One homeowner's earliest purchase was a primitive wooden cupboard. Its blue buttermilk paint inspired other purchases, including a stack of handmade storage boxes. As a collection, old boxes, which have been used since Early American times, hold great appeal. Not only do they lend character to shelves or a desktop, but they are handy. They even look great piled on the floor. And the more they are used, the better they get.

Knowing the history of the items in such a collection always adds to its enjoyment. Before glass jars, tin cans, and commercially packaged foods, wooden boxes made by local carpenters served almost every household need. Candle boxes, matchboxes, and boxes for sugar, cheese, cornmeal, grains, and butter were a dime a dozen (or rather two to fifteen shillings).

As early as the seventeenth century, boxes were cataloged along with household belongings. The identification of items on a box, such as spices or silverware, told much about the possessions of a particular household. Accountings of such, found in wills and inventory books, often noted them and provide insight into how people lived in the seventeenth, eighteenth, and nineteenth centuries.

A great number of boxes, and their contents, were imported in exchange

A couple turned their personal passion for all things rustic and Western into a unique and comfortable home in the Berkshires. Their collections include Navajo blankets and baskets. The family gathers regularly at a 7-foot-long trestle table from the 1920s.

large carved boxes made especially for this purpose. Certain kinds of foods had their specific boxes as well. No self-respecting gentleman was without his snuff box, while a proper young lady had her box to hold a paint set. Aristocracy had silver eyepatch boxes of all sizes and shapes. Money, too, was usually kept in a locked box. Large carved combs were quite popular in the 1830s, and boxes were made to fit them.

While it once may have been necessary to keep things in boxes due to lack of

for the American-made products sent overseas. For example, ladies' sewing implements were imported from England in the late 1700s, as were gentlemen's shaving kits—all neatly packaged in elaborate boxes.

From the 1600s to the early nineteenth century, almost all household goods were stored in boxes in one manner or another. For example, clothing, bed linens, tablecloths, and napkins were stored in

HOUSEHOLD HINTS

The following are some tips for keeping household tasks to a minimum and putting them to work as part of the decorating scheme:

1. An upholstered headboard can be covered in a white cotton slipcover that's washed, then buttoned back on while still slightly damp. There's no need to iron: Fabrics stretch back to shape, and wrinkles smooth themselves out while drying.
2. Replace pillow and quilt covers when just washed and barely damp. The fabric will look extra soft after it dries.
3. Add your own vintage trims to store-bought pillowcases for a personal touch to furnishing. You don't have to spend much for a great look.

CAST IRON

Cast iron is basically iron that is poured into a mold to create useful implements, such as pots and pans, and muffin tins. Cast-iron cookware was highly valued in the eighteenth century. George Washington's mother thought so much of her cookware that she made a special bequeath of her cast iron in her will. Lewis and Clark indicated that their cast iron Dutch oven was one of their most important pieces of equipment during their expedition in the Louisiana territory in 1804.

An old storage chest and a collection of wicker bags provides ample storage for winter scarves, gloves, and hats.

Big bens and baby bens by Westclox and the French maker Jaz line the top shelf. Apothecary jars in amber and clear glass are mostly European. Large glass containers are filled with collected shells that sit among larger shells and coral on the bottom shelf.

drawer space or too few closets, boxes are still quite appealing to those who like things neat and tidy.

Other everyday items make great collectibles as well. Vintage kitchenware, including pots, pans, and smaller cooking tools and utensils, creates atmosphere simply hanging from a space-saving rack. And a plant stand can get a new life as a plate holder with a fresh coat of white paint.

The fireplace was built of indigenous stone. The stack of painted firkins is a favorite collection.

In the kitchen, an English hutch displays kitchen-related collectibles, including canisters and canning jars, antique scales from around the world, French coffee grinders, signage, and wall clocks.

In the family room, a carefully curated landscape of cameras, binoculars, and field glasses from the late 1800s to the 1940s is united by theme.

Vintage signs create visual interest in this black and white kitchen.

PEWTER

Pewter is an alloy predominately composed of tin and was formulated as a less expensive alternative to silver. It was used primarily for tableware in the early nineteenth century, when porcelain was introduced. It is still produced today, but mainly for decorative items. Pewter items such as spoons, plates, and beer steins are often found in antique shops; their color, shape, and history make for an interesting, affordable collection.

Many collectors of old pewter let it darken to look old. However, the original pieces found in eighteenth- and nineteenth-century households were routinely polished to keep them bright and shiny. When pewter is used, it is washed and dried often and usually stays in good condition. If you want to keep your pewter pieces looking good, it is best to use them as often as possible.

A marvelous collection of nineteenth-century pewter serving pieces and spoons are displayed on a painted hanging tavern shelf.

EARLY AMERICAN GRAPHIC SIGNS

Accessories such as folk art, old signage, and Americana punch up any environment. When decorating with these objects, try to arrange them so their shapes complement one another. Early graphic signs made of wood, tin, or paper hung as art provide visual interest in any room. They are quite affordable and have become popular vintage accessories. You can also find reproductions that look just like the originals—no one will be the wiser.

America's golden age of sign making occurred from the last quarter of the eighteenth century to the mid-nineteenth century. Signs were usually hung on storefronts and advertised the businesses within; they were often comprised of a

Graphic signs make wonderful pieces of artwork in any style room.

large image and a few words. White pine was the wood of choice because it was plentiful, easy to carve, and durable in all types of weather.

Antique shops dealing in folk art are the best source for wooden trade signs. Early tavern signs are the most plentiful and are among the favorites. They often depict an American eagle, a bull, or a horse. Collectors should be aware that the date on a tavern sign represents when the innkeeper received his license, not necessarily the date the sign was made.

Putty-colored walls and white woodwork prove a reliable foundation for bright linens and funky signs discovered at a local flea-market.

PHOTOGRAPHIC COLLECTIONS

It has always been fashionable to hang framed photographs as art. A collection of turn-of-the-century photos of children, or a group of black-and-white portraits, for example, make charming subjects and give a home character. Antique shops often sell old photo albums for just a few dollars, and you can selectively pair the most artistic photos with random frames. Of course, displaying them in an artistic manner is what makes it work.

Sepia-Tone Photographs

Many old photographs were printed with sepia ink extracted from cuttlefish. (The term sepia tone refers to a photograph printed in brown scale rather than gray scale.) The resulting image is a monotone in shades of brown. Such photographs evoke times gone by.

Opposite page: Weathered signage and industrial elements provide wall art in a vintage kitchen.

Below: A grouping of black-and-white vintage photographs of women who convey confidence and strength is used to create a theme.

Before the advent of color photography, photographers often used a sepia bath to create gentler lines and a softer appearance, especially for portraits. As the photograph fades with time, the deep brown of the sepia leaches out, leaving a fading image behind. Depending on where the photograph was kept and whether or not it was exposed to sunlight, it may start to yellow or develop strong red tones. When these pictures were new, they would have been tinted in rich shades of brown.

Early sepia photographs are paired with a variety of vintage frames for a soft, subdued collection. It's interesting to incorporate the history of others into your own home.

A shelf holds all sorts of memorabilia from the past in subtle shades of neutral.

A collection of reproduction antique maps is divided into separate frames for an interesting treatment.

CREATIVE ARRANGEMENTS

Most collections are highly personal and often are not secured for their monetary value, but because they represent an expression of particular interest to the collector.

By using a minimal palette, you can learn to arrange an abundance of "stuff" in an orderly way. Well-organized exhibits in black, cream, and gold frames, for example, will enable you to incorporate the history of others into your own home. These might include such relics as pocket diaries and souvenirs, and candid photographs you find.

Or you might be the sort of homeowner/collector who likes your space visually simple and organized. Moving things around until everything looks right can become a passion. The following are a few basic rules for creating compositions:

1. Define the space with a large architectural element, such as a frame or mirror, before working in smaller objects.
2. Stick to a basic palette of two or three colors, and then add a punchy accent color.
3. Use what you love. Every object should have visual and emotional resonance for you.

INDEX

PHOTOGRAPHY CREDITS

Front Cover: Alf Ertsland/iStockphoto

Back Cover (clockwise from top right): Laura Moss,
   Keith Scott Morton, Steven Randazzo.
   Background: Alf Ertsland/iStockphoto

Endpapers: Jens Carsten Rosemann/iStockphoto

Pierre Chanteau: 48, 56 top, 106

Philip Clayton-Thompson: II-III, 11, 50, 73 right, 91 bottom,
   112-113

Jonn Coolidge: 57 left, 58-59, 60

Grey Crawford: 7 (both photos), 23-25, 103 top, 147, 171
   bottom

Susie Cushner: 62, 64

Miki Duisterhof: 2, 14 bottom right, 15-17, 49, 79, 88 top left,
   101, 102, 103 bottom, 118-119, 122 top, 123, 130 left, 135,
   137, 142

Don Freeman: 13

Thayer Allyson Gowdy: 54

Gridley + Graves: 8, 46, 47 (all photos), 56 bottom, 75 bottom,
   80, 96, 105 top, 116

Aimee Herring: 97 top

Keller + Keller: V bottom, 27-29, 63, 88 top right, 95, 132, 145,
   170

Robert Kent: X, 5, 6, 90 (both photos), 91 top, 92 (both
   photos), 94, 105 bottom, 107, 109, 156

Michael Luppino: IIII bottom, V top, 39, 70-71, 81 bottom, 100

Andrew McCaul: 67, 97 bottom

Ellen McDermott: IIII top, 38, 40-45, 55, 104, 122 bottom, 124
   bottom, 126-127, 166 left, 168-169, 172, 175

Keith Scott Morton: VI, IX, 3, 9, 14 left, 19, 20-21, 31-37, 52,
   66, 68-69, 74, 75 top, 76-78, 81 top, 82, 83, 85, 86, 88 bottom
   right, 89, 93, 114, 115, 117, 121, 125, 128, 131, 133, 136, 138,
   140 top, 141 right, 144, 148 right, 149-150, 152 bottom, 153,
   155 right, 164, 171 top

Olde Good Things: 72 bottom

Peta Smyth Antique Textiles: 73 left

Steven Randazzo: 10, 72 top, 98, 99, 108, 139, 141 left, 161-163,
   165, 166 right, 167, 173, 174 (both photos)

Laura Resen: 130 right, 140 bottom

Charles Schiller: 157, 159 (all photos)

William P. Steele: 4, 57 right, 111, 134, 160

Robin Stubbert: 30, 53, 120, 124 top, 148 left, 151, 152 top, 154,
   155 left

Simon Upton: 61

Andreas von Einsiedel (interior design by Alexandra Stoddard):
   14 top right, 143, 146

Paul Whicheloe: 84

Design by Renato Stanisic

Library of Congress Cataloging-in-Publication Data

Linsley, Leslie.
  Aged to perfection : adding rustic charm to your modern home inside & out / Leslie Linsley.
     p. cm.
  Includes index.
  ISBN 978-1-58816-773-6
  1. Decoration and ornament, Rustic. 2. Interior decoration--United States--History--21st century. I. Title.
  NK1994.R87L56 2010
  747--dc22
                              2010003997

10 9 8 7 6 5 4 3

Published by Hearst Books
A division of Sterling Publishing Co., Inc.
387 Park Avenue South, New York, NY 10016

Country Living is a registered trademark of Hearst Communications, Inc.

www.countryliving.com

For information about custom editions, special sales, premium and corporate purchases, please contact Sterling Special Sales Department at 800-805-5489 or specialsales@sterlingpublishing.com.

Distributed in Canada by Sterling Publishing
C/o Canadian Manda Group, 165 Dufferin Street
Toronto, Ontario, Canada M6K 3H6

Distributed in Australia by Capricorn Link (Australia) Pty. Ltd.
P.O. Box 704, Windsor, NSW 2756 Australia

Manufactured in China

Sterling ISBN 978-1-58816-773-6